ESSAYS ON INTERVENTION

A Publication of the
Mershon Center for Education in National Security

Essays on Intervention

Roger Fisher
Richard A. Falk
Michael H. Cardozo
William T. Burke

Edited by Roland J. Stanger

OHIO STATE UNIVERSITY PRESS

1964

Foreword

OUR SOCIETY is primarily organized territorially, in terms of states traditionally described as sovereign and independent. Theoretically each state is responsible for determining the policies which are to prevail within its borders. States have none the less commonly tried to influence the course of events in other states, where their writ does not run. Certainly not all such interventionary actions are censurable. Some are even affirmatively desirable. They are, in any event, inevitable, given the always limited and progressively diminishing relevance of national boundaries to economic activity, military strategy, social problems, artistic expression, religious belief, and ideological commitment. States with expansionist tendencies have, however, indulged in interventionary actions not justifiable by any reasonable standard. So have states committed to the status quo in a changing world. Among the significant factors characterizing such acts have been the kind and degree of coercion used, usually the threat or use of armed force. Extreme coercion is not only often destructive of material and other values, but poses the risk of expanded conflict.

The balance of power system which prevailed before World War I had certain built-in stabilizing elements which discouraged both interventionary actions and the expansion of such conflicts as did occur. The bipolar world which is the product of the two world wars lacks those stabilizing elements. Every change in orientation of any of the other powers is seen as adding to the strength of one of the superpowers and detracting from that of the other. Hence each superpower feels compelled to use every means to hold its allies, to wean away the other's allies, to woo each uncommitted nation—and to counter its opponent's every like move. By the same token, every conflict inherently tends to expand into a larger conflict. A complicating though by no means unfortunate development is the introduction into the international arena of a multitude of supranational organizations, formal and informal, with varying roles and potentials.

Drawing a clear line between permissible and impermissible interventionary acts, never easy but always desirable, is now both harder and much more urgent. The papers in this volume are addressed to that problem.

A striking feature of these essays, having in mind their different subjects and the individual approaches of the authors, is the consensus they reflect regarding basic issues and solutions. All are agreed that the standards of customary international law relating to intervention are ambiguous, confused, outdated and inadequate. William T. Burke's challenging analysis suggests the many factors that need to be taken into account in formulating more relevant and precise standards. A second recurring theme is that the line between internal strife and international conflict has not only become more difficult to draw, but is now less significant with reference to the basic concern, threats to the peace. Struggles among competing factions for internal supremacy are too often seen, both by the participants and abroad, as facets of a larger conflict between the white and colored races, or between the privileged and underprivileged, or in terms of anticolonialism, to permit viewing them as of only domestic concern. And too often, for these or other reasons, these struggles become enmeshed in the cold war, perhaps only because one of the superpowers chooses to invest its resources and prestige in the outcome. Brooding over the whole scene is the ominous threat of nuclear war, and the risks that interventionary acts create that the threat may materialize—the risks of war by escalation, accident or miscalculation, and of catalytic war.

Perhaps most remarkably, it is common ground in these essays that community action, normally through the United Nations, is often the appropriate response to the problems created by the irresistible pressures for change in the world and the risks of unilateral intervention. Roger Fisher urges that "all the rules about intervention are meaningless if every nation can decide for itself which governments are legitimate and how to characterize particular limited conflict." He suggests that recognition of the existence of a state or of a government should be a community decision. He would also give to the United Nations the responsibility for characterizing conflicts as involving internal lawlessness, domestic revolution, or foreign attack. He pleads also for a policy requiring non-forceful intervention to be reasonably related to the ends sought. Richard A. Falk imaginatively proposes recognition of the authority of the United Nations to engage in "legislative intervention" to coerce domestic social changes whenever civil strife threatens world peace or whenever gross abuses of human rights exist. He views the legitimacy of intervention as depending in part on whether it is unilateral, multilateral, regional or universal, through the United Nations, and in part on whether it is based on principles that express patterns of general community consent. He believes intervention by the United Nations on a selective basis is a preferable alternative to destructive and indecisive symmetrical intervention by nuclear rivals. Michael H. Cardozo, although his subject is that seemingly most benign form of intervention, the provision of economic assistance, likewise proposes using international agencies to channel such assistance to needy states. Aid is commonly offered subject to conditions, but there are conditions related to the purposes of the program and conditions imposed to advantage the donor. He suggests that channeling aid through international agencies, as in the case of UNRRA, both ensures against conditions with a nationalistic hue and protects the donor states from the political onus of exacting necessary but unpopular conditions from aid recipients.

Three of the essays included herein were originally presented at the Ohio State University at a Regional Meeting of the American Society of International Law. It has become a tradition for the College of Law and the Mershon Committee on Education in National Security annually to co-sponsor a regional meeting on the campus.

This book is published by the Committee in order that these essays may find a wider audience.

ROLAND J. STANGER
Professor of Law
Ohio State University

Contents

ESSAYS ON INTERVENTION

Intervention: Three Problems of Policy and Law

ROGER FISHER *

EVERYONE recognizes that the problem of intervention involves questions both of policy and of law, but there is disagreement as to how the two are to be distinguished and how they are related. The very question of how one ought to perceive the relationship between international law and international policy is itself a matter of policy. This paper is intended to illustrate one working approach to that policy question, first by some general remarks and then by discussion of three problems.

Some international lawyers prefer to sweep all policy issues into a determination of what is lawful. They consider rules of law as handy indexes to policy considerations and to the accumulated wisdom of the past. By reviewing these in the light of an exhaustive check list of considerations, one decides what course of action

---

* Professor of Law, Harvard University.

is reasonable. If it is reasonable then, by definition, it is legal. Under this view, law is not regarded as a restraint on behavior, a restraint which it might sometimes be reasonable to break. At least in the international area it would never be reasonable to break the law, for if the conduct were reasonable it would be lawful.

Others of us prefer to consider policy considerations as having a dual role. Policy is taken into account in determining what is the law, but only to the extent consistent with a legal tradition reflecting well-known canons of statutory construction and judicial restraint. Under this view a judge, or anyone else deciding what the law is, behaves as though his decision were determined by objective rules interpreted in an objective way. The framing of laws should, but decisions according to law should not, take everything into account. The goddess of justice is regularly pictured as being blindfolded, representing this limitation on what should be considered. The policy benefits that follow from deciding questions with judicial restraint and by reference to objective rules are deemed to outweigh the benefits that follow from acting like Solomon and deciding each question afresh as a policy matter. When I speak of law I use the word in this non-McDougal sense. I mean rules and norms of conduct determined by methods approaching traditional legal analysis. Defining law in this way results in there being some policy considerations not embodied in the law in a particular case.

This traditional conception of law seems particularly

4

useful in the international area, for it helps to focus attention on the gap between what a country believes the law to be and what it believes it is wise or reasonable to do. In a domestic court it is enough to persuade a judge of what the law is. Once he has been persuaded of the law he need not be given further reasons why he ought to follow it. The question, "Ought this court to follow the law?" simply does not arise. This is true of the lowest state court and of the Supreme Court of the United States. With rare exceptions, it is also true of non-judicial governmental officials. An assistant may be asked by the Postmaster General for a memorandum on his constitutional or statutory powers to seize a book. The Postmaster General does not ask for a memorandum on whether or not he should exceed his powers. If he thinks that sound policy requires that he have additional powers, he will seek to have the law changed.

In the domestic scene this is belaboring the obvious. We have a government of laws and not of men. But if we shift our sights to the international arena it is not only not obvious, it is not true. Seldom is it enough to persuade the Secretary of State or a presidential assistant that a proposed course of action would violate international law. He will want to know also whether the law should be observed. He will often accept a statement as to the rules of international law but believe that it is wise or reasonable to break the rules. As the law looks to him, and as it looks to me, there exists outside the law a policy question: "Should the law be respected?"

5

The rules of international law are often less precise than the rules of domestic law. There is a great deal of room for refinement and clarification, work which should, of course, take into account the conflicting substantive interests involved. But the clarification of rules does not exhaust the problem. We must also worry about that possible gap between what looks legal to a government official and what looks reasonable to him. Some may try to close the gap by telling the official that whatever he finds to be reasonable, is legal. It strikes me as wiser, and likely to be more helpful in producing international order, to start from the other end—to make an objective and traditional lawyer-like determination of what is the rule of international law, and then seek to persuade the official to follow it. In my view, legality, like honesty, has objective qualities. To persuade a decision-maker that international legality is the best policy, like trying to persuade him that honesty is the best policy, is a useful task. If successfully done it will tend to produce order. On the other hand, to try to persuade an international decision-maker that whatever is reasonable is legal, is like trying to persuade him that whatever is the best policy is honest. It is not a useful task. If successfully done it will tend to produce disorder.

Rules of law must be related not only to the policies they are designed to serve, but also to the means by which compliance with the rules is to be sought. For the foreseeable future the basic means by which compliance with international law may be obtained is through the enlightened self-interest of the various

6

governments. If this is so, we must be prepared to argue that respect for international rules does in fact serve the interest of each government. The most fruitful perspective from which to discuss a question of international law may, therefore, be the one which seeks to persuade a government official of what a government ought to do.

Should We Intervene by Force in Response to Intervention by Force?

A central question in the conduct of international affairs is that of the use of armed force by one country within the territory of another. Although there is much room for discussion, the basic rules of international law are reasonably clear. In the United Nations Charter all members undertook to refrain in their international relations from the threat or use of force against the territorial integrity or political independence of any state. One can go beyond this. It is illegal for one country to use armed force within the territory of another against the will of its legitimate government. On the other hand, with the consent of the legitimate government, other countries may lend military assistance either to defend it against foreign attack or to help it maintain internal law and order—up to the point where it is threatened with revolution. If a government is threatened by an internal and potentially successful revolution it is the duty of other governments to stand aside.[1] Even if, as in Hungary, the existing government invites assistance from another nation, a popular revolution should be permitted to run its course without outside interference. The United States, which was established through revolution, has always recognized that right in others.

One might start with the preliminary question of whether the United States would like a world in which these rules were respected by all, or whether it would prefer a world in which force was generally used to settle disputes. In discussion of disarmament, some people appear to take a position which is fundamentally an assertion that the United States' objectives can best be achieved—or can only be achieved—in a world in which might is right. They seem to believe that the ideas and institutions which explain our existence as a nation can make their way in the world only if they are emblazoned on regimental banners. A sufficient answer to this belief is the danger of such international anarchy in a nuclear age. A premise of this paper is that the United States would prefer a world in which all countries respected the basic rules against intervention to a world in which all countries did not.

One other premise needs to be stated. The United States cannot expect to engage in forceful intervention itself and at the same time have all other governments refrain. In isolated cases, it might be possible to carry out secretly a limited program of forceful interference in other nations' affairs. But in a democracy any continuing policy of sending significant intervening forces into other countries could not be kept secret for long. Faced with such conduct by the United States, totalitarian governments, which may more easily act in secret and more easily justify immediate actions by reference to remote goals, could be expected quickly to follow our example.

Neither of these assumptions is often challenged by government officials. The disagreement arises when we have to decide on a response to another nation's act of intervention. It is in this situation that an official is likely to murmur pointedly that our observance of the Queensberry Rules does not seem to keep our opponents from hitting below the belt, and to ask whether we should not do better to imitate them. Examining the question, the official will discover that there are alternative courses of conduct: to respond with intervention of our own or, refraining from intervention, to adhere to international law and try to bring pressure to bear on other nations to do likewise.

A policy of subversive intervention by the United States is subject to serious handicaps. It may be, as our officials seem to believe, that the officials of totalitarian governments proceed by making Machiavellian assessments of what they can get away with, without regard to moral restraints on private or national conduct. I, for one, do not believe that this is so. The human need to feel that what one is doing is somehow the right thing to do is not a uniquely American or Western trait. I think the first step toward international understanding is to realize that officials of other countries regard themselves as good people, pursuing proper ends by legitimate means. But whether this is true of all nations or not, it is clear that the conduct of the United States and other free nations is subject

9

to both moral and political restraints. Our officials could not, even if they wished, embark on a program of political assassinations or mass terrorism of noncombatants in a time of peace. Such restraints limit the possibilities of intervention; they do not prohibit it altogether. There are ways of intervening that are open to us if the objective to be served is, or is thought to be, important enough. But it remains true that a general disregard of the obligation not to intervene will be less advantageous to the United States than to nations which, by our standards, are less squeamish.

More generally, the international situation which presently confronts us is not one in which a United States policy of intervention is likely to be successful. In the West, such a policy might conceivably extend the reach of democracy. Forceful subversion might enable us occasionally to replace a dictatorship with a democratic regime. But attempts to give illegal support to revolutionary movements in Spain, Portugal, and Latin America, for example, would be immediately and seriously disruptive of existing arrangements for military and economic co-operation. The certain loss in these areas is not recovered in a possibility, tenuous at best, of revolutionary success. Moreover, even if that possibility were realized, the questions would remain whether the establishment of democracy would be permanent and, if it were, what our relations would be with a new government anxious to test its strength. Even if these doubts could be overcome, we should be left with the dilemma of separating governments which are "satisfactory" from those which are not and,

10

with respect to the latter, of choosing among rival revolutionary groups.

In the Communist world, subversive intervention offers even less promise of success. Covert action by the United States within the Soviet Union or the countries within its orbit appears more likely to solidify resistance to change than to bring about a counter-revolution. Even in Cuba, beyond the reach of Soviet ground forces, the possibility of undermining the Castro regime by giving subversive support to Cuban rebels is remote. Attempts in that direction will, in the long run, probably seem comparable to giving support to Chiang's dream of recapturing the Chinese mainland. Internal change in nations where communism is now established depends almost entirely on the attitude of the people there. It depends on their national goals and on what we can tell them about our part of the world, not on the necessarily sporadic support which we might give to underground movements. To be sure, in a particular case, such support might have marginal utility in pushing back the iron curtain, but this possibility must be considered with the greatest skepticism.

Active participation in subversive movements by the United States would remove whatever inhibitions the Communist nations now feel against engaging in subversive conduct. We would, in effect, be discarding the rules altogether because our opponents observe them less fully than do we. But if it is true that we are up against "bad men" who seize every opportunity to achieve their objectives, this is like throwing Br'er Rabbit into the briar patch.

The situation which I have pictured is a discouraging and frustrating one. Communist governments engage in subversive activities and make some gains. If we respond in kind we gain little and increase the possibility of further intervention—and further gains—on their side.

Such considerations cannot demonstrate that seeking to counter subversive intervention by engaging in it ourselves will in fact do more harm than good. They do suggest that a policy of responding with counter-subversion has comparatively little to offer and runs the risk of causing the United States to suffer a net loss. The second alternative, a policy of adhering to international law and trying to cause other nations to do likewise, may well offer greater hope of success.

Simply to refrain from intervention ourselves is not likely to produce restraint in other governments. Our bad example will surely be followed; our good example, by itself, will not. A successful policy must not only avoid providing an excuse for forceful intervention; it must tend to induce other nations to lessen their subversive activities. It must decrease the possibility of gain from subversion and increase the cost of the gamble. In such a policy, international law can play a central role.

Efforts to frustrate foreign subversion by supporting a local government are legal under international law, unless the government is faced with a genuine local revolution—which, by definition, is not a problem of foreign intervention. At the invitation of the local government, as is the case of the United States in South

Vietnam, almost all means which the United States might use within South Vietnam to counter intervention are permitted by international law. Not only military but intelligence personnel may be made available to friendly governments to help them deter or track down and capture saboteurs, assassins, and others who may be operating within their borders on behalf of a foreign government.

But such direct measures designed to decrease the gains of subversion should be accompanied by clarification of the rules of international law if we are to increase the political cost to other nations of engaging in illegal subversive intervention. This requires clarification of the rules and the facts.

One significant feature of governments is that they feel compelled to justify what they do according to principle. We should make the most of this. We should also recognize that any government that spends vast amounts on propaganda is one which considers public opinion important and is likely to recognize that public actions speak louder than words. A major aspect of the present contest between East and West is the struggle for popular support among politically active people throughout the rest of the world. It costs a country some of its support every time it becomes obvious that it is breaking the rules it professes.

World public opinion is not all-important. It can certainly be outweighed by other considerations. Even more relevant to our problem is the fact that there can be a great deal of difference between one kind of adverse public opinion and another. On some occasions, for example, an adverse reaction simply reflects a general wish that the action had not been taken. This may have been true with respect to the neutral reaction to the Soviet resumption of nuclear testing in the fall of 1961. On other occasions, however, an adverse reaction reveals a radical change of beliefs and attitudes by a particularly significant group. It may reflect complete dismay at the Communist system or a rude awakening as to what a Communist government is really like. This was the kind of reaction which followed the brutal Russian suppression of the Hungarian revolution. That action caused many members of the Communist party in various countries to resign from the party. The Soviet Union paid a heavy and meaningful price for its intervention, a price it will not want to pay often.

If we are to expect such a price for noncompliance with the international law of intervention, we shall have to clarify the rules beyond the basic propositions stated above. We must sharpen our theory of what the law ought to be. If, as here urged, we conclude that the best policy is to respect the rules even though others do not, we should do what we can to develop an international consensus to that effect. We should develop criteria for distinguishing between a revolutionary group that has some outside support and foreign subversion that has some domestic support. We should be able to state how far assistance to a friendly government is compatible with the recognition of the right to revolt. The formulation of at least tentative answers to questions such as these is a pressing task

14

facing us if we are to develop a policy guided by rules of international law. And in order to make it understood that this is our policy, we must state clearly what rules we ourselves are following.

The next step is to make every attempt to raise the rules which we propose, or these rules as modified by the proposals of other nations, to a position of general acceptance among the nations of the world. Our adherence to law will be such in name only unless we are prepared to recognize the views of others entitled to an equal voice in developing these rules.

In his April 22, 1961, message to President Kennedy concerning the American role in the attack on Cuba, Premier Khrushchev said: "We consider that any interference by one state in the affairs of another, especially armed interference, is a violation of all international laws."[2] It is easy to find other statements by Russian and Chinese Communists proclaiming the importance of non-intervention and their respect for international law. One is tempted to dismiss these words as merely words, confident that they are camouflage for acts of intervention over the globe. But although skepticism about Russian sincerity is justified, we should not forget that the lack of any standards for defining intervention makes it hard for us as well as for them to know how to characterize a situation. In any event, we should use the pronouncements of the Russians and Chinese, sincere or not, to emphasize the law of intervention, and as a basis for clarifying it. There are so many different situations around the world—from Eastern Europe to Africa to Latin America—that it might be possible to articulate some genuinely neutral principles of law. Even if not, the attempt to do so would bring into sharper focus the fact that some involvements in the affairs of other nations are lawful and some are not, and thereby put pressure on every nation to state in each case the general principle to which it adheres which justifies its conduct.

In addition to clarifying the law, every attempt should be made to ascertain and publicize the facts in situations where one side or another is accused of unlawful intervention. In many cases, international fact-finding bodies have proved an effective means to this end. Where this device is impractical, the United States should consider the discovery and publication of documented facts a primary objective. A well-prepared White Paper can have an impact far beyond that of bare assertions of intervention no matter how true they may be.

Let me illustrate the central policy role which the clarification of law and facts might play with the present situation in Vietnam. In South Vietnam, as elsewhere, the United States is attempting to reduce the effect of subversive Communist intervention by assisting broad programs of economic and social reform. We provide technical and military assistance directed specifically at the problem of subversion. Such measures are an important part of our foreign policy. They significantly reduce the possibility of gain from subversive intervention. But unless we can distinguish both for ourselves and for others our intervention in support of the Vietnamese government from the ac-

16

tivities of the Viet Cong in South Vietnam, showing the former to be lawful and the latter not, we expose ourselves to charges of colonialism and domination,[3] and make it easier for the Viet Cong to increase its activities. Assuming that South and North Vietnam are now to be regarded as separate nations, we should, as an essential element of even our military measures to frustrate Communist intervention in South Vietnam, expose and publicize the distinction between our activities, solicited by the Vietnamese government, and the infiltration of Communist forces from the north.

Like the United States, the communist nations are heavily engaged in an attempt to win the support of the uncommitted nations. They are concerned to cement loose ties which they now have with other nations and to weaken ties which different, and often the same, nations have with the United States. In this contest it is important that the United States exact the full price in loss of popular support for Communist acts of illegal intervention. The reaction may not often be comparable to the aftermath of Hungary, but this does not mean that the price for lesser intervention is insignificant. That the Communists do not regard it as insignificant is attested by statements like that of the Chinese foreign ministry, charging the United States with "intervention and aggression"[4] in South Vietnam. The success of our lawful activities in opposition to Communist subversion depends in large measure on our ability to forestall such propaganda by making clear the facts of each situation and the rule of international law which applies. On such ability depends also the

17

prevention of unlawful Communist activity, or at least a lessening of the net gains which can be achieved from it. If we cannot make lawlessness so costly as to yield a net loss, we surely can reduce the profit significantly.

By such a blending of law and policy I would hope to persuade officials of our government that the United States should not intervene by force in violation of existing international law even though other governments do. In the harsh reality of today's world we have few enough weapons. Law, and the deference to principle which governments necessarily profess, are weapons which we should use with skill and understanding.

Should We Decide for Ourselves Which Rule of Intervention Applies?

A second big problem in the law of intervention is that of characterizing the factual situation. Even if countries agree on the rules, there remains the difficult question of applying the rules to the facts. As a policy matter, what method should the United States use for deciding whether a particular situation is a revolution, a case of foreign aggression, or a case of internal disorder?

In South Vietnam, both sides are receiving support from other nations. To the extent that the legitimacy of external support for one side depends on the fact that the other side receives such support, the possibility of an escalating situation in which nations give an increasing amount of what they regard as lawful assist-

18

ance to their favored contender can be avoided only if it is clear which is *the* legitimate government in South Vietnam. Similarly, the lawfulness of support for one side or another may depend on where you start. Should the Viet Cong guerrillas who remained in South Vietnam after the Geneva settlement of 1954 be considered as invaders from North Vietnam, or are they now to be regarded as South Vietnamese, attempting to reform their government? Is Katanga a part of the Congo or an independent state with the right of self-determination? At the root of the difficulty is the problem of recognition.

In recent years, the United States has taken the position that recognition of a government or state is a political act within the unlimited discretion of each government. We have steadfastly refused to recognize the government of China, continuing to operate as if Chiang and his officials on Taiwan constituted that government. So long as we reserve the right to base international legal relationships on a policy of recognition that ignores reality, we must accept the assertion of the same right by other nations. But this permits the Soviet Union to recognize a Communist Viet Cong government as the legitimate government of South Vietnam, which it could then lawfully assist in resisting the government which we recognize and support. Bluntly, all the rules about intervention are meaningless if every nation can decide for itself which governments are legitimate and how to characterize particular limited conflict. Unless we are prepared to continue a situation in which the legality of intervention will often depend on which side of the fence you are on, and in which, therefore, our policy necessarily becomes one of countering force with force, we must be willing to refer questions of recognition and characterization of a disorder to some authority other than ourselves. The United Nations is the most likely candidate for this role.

We should not expect Charter revision in the immediate future. But imaginative use of the existing United Nations machinery could probably meet the problem. The recognition problem could be resolved by U.N. admission procedures, combined with the question of credentials. Most of the world is in the United Nations. The question of the legitimacy of a government can in these circumstances usually be answered by its status in the U.N. For this to be effective, however, the United States must reverse its current position that recognition is a political decision which each government can take unilaterally. We should shift to the position that the existence of a state or the existence of a government is a community decision, to be taken in the light of the facts. Such recognition need not signify approval of the regime any more than the *de facto* recognition of a corporation connotes government approval of its products.

The United States might be prepared to accept recommendations to member states by a two-thirds vote of the General Assembly that a particular government be accepted as the government of a designated territory. This could be our standard. The example of Katanga suggests that the General Assembly will not always come out on the side of independence for every unit that may seek self-determination. To be sure, there is merit in the current American position that recognition is a political question. The difficulty lies in the consequences of different governments reaching different decisions. Like the United States, the General Assembly may make a political decision as to which government ought to be recognized. But the decision would be nonetheless useful for being political.

In addition to the problem of characterizing governments there is the problem of characterizing conflicts. Is it a domestic revolution, requiring other governments to stay out, or is it a case of internal lawlessness or foreign attack, in which all governments may help the recognized government and none may help the insurgents? Here, again, the General Assembly by resolution could recommend the appropriate action.

The suggestion that the United States refer such questions to the United Nations and follow the decision of the General Assembly meets a number of fundamental criticisms. Strong voices in the Senate have recently renewed the complaint that the United States is deferring too often to the views of the United Nations. In answering such criticisms international lawyers and government officials should have a clear conception of what our basic international policies are, where these will be furthered by seeking and accepting United Nations determinations, as, I think, is the case with determinations of status, and where they will not.

At the present time the United States is prepared to fight for the principle that countries should not suffer from what the United States considers to be aggression. It is a good and honorable principle. It is not unlike the principle that within this country both the federal and state governments will act to see that the people do not suffer from unconstitutional conduct. But within this country it has been found wise to institutionalize the process for deciding what is unconstitutional. In fact, an institutionalized decision is essential if we are to avoid a head-on conflict between governments which view the situation differently, each defending the principle as it sees it. For the state of Louisiana or the executive branch of the federal government to defend the Constitution as it is interpreted by others is not to abandon principled behavior. Similarly, to defer to the United Nations on such questions as which is the legitimate government of a country is not to abandon principle. On the contrary, it is to accept the principle that the legitimate government of a country may better be deemed to be that government which is thought to be so by two-thirds of the countries of the world than that which is thought to be so by the United States.

But, some will say, the United Nations might determine that South Vietnam was subject to an internal revolution and that the United States should withhold all assistance. To accept such a United Nations determination might mean the loss of one more country to communism. It might. But one cannot repeat too often that the United States is not fighting to subject

South Vietnam to American control. We are engaged in carrying out a painful and unpleasant duty, and one which we may not be able to carry out successfully. We are fighting to defend the rules of decent conduct toward people. We can do more to maintain those rules by not insisting that we should be the judge in every case.

This does not mean that we should refer every decision to the United Nations or follow their recommendation on every issue. But in the determination of which is the legitimate government and in the characterization of limited conflict we have more to gain by accepting and urging others to accept a United Nations decision than by reaching an individual decision. If the General Assembly recommends that the United States disarm or refrain from particular action, we should not feel bound by it. The United States ought not to determine its foreign policy by deciding what would make the United Nations happy. Far from it. But where particular questions of status require a uniform decision throughout the world, we should appreciate the virtue of having an institution make the decision. Rather than insist upon defending the international community against aggression as defined by us, we can seek to defend it against aggression as defined by the clear majority of that community—a policy which should equally well defend us, which might have more chance of success, and which should lessen the critical problem of plausibly legitimate intervention on both sides of a local war.

*What Restraints Should We Respect on the Use of
Pressure Short of Force?*

Talk of the general problem of the use of coercion by
one government against another tends to confuse two
drastically different questions under the single label
"intervention." At the very time that the government
of South Vietnam requested thousands of American
soldiers to come into its country to help defend the
regime, it objected to the United States' meddling
in its "internal" affairs. South Vietnam obviously considered the two questions separable. So did the United
States. It was reported that the United States decision
to step up military intervention was coupled with a
decision "de-emphasizing the necessity for the reform
of President Diem's autocratic and often capricious
regime."[5] What are the international guidelines with
respect to one government's concerning itself with the
domestic affairs of another?

Much attention in the past has been devoted to the
degree of "domesticity" of the question in which the
foreign government is interested, but such a test can
hardly determine the propriety of action by other
governments. Internal matters are sometimes of legitimate concern to other countries. On the other hand
some international matters, such as a vote at the
United Nations, should probably be free from foreign
coercion. Certainly a boycott by a major power designed to bring about a particular vote in the Security
Council by a smaller country would be highly objectionable. Further, neither the kind nor the intensity

of coercion (short of armed force, or threats of force) automatically makes it subject to legitimate criticism.

There appears to be little law to date in this area. Most of the issues are ones of reason and politics. The United States is not required by international law to aid a particular country, or to allow American citizens to travel there, or to buy goods from that country; it would seem that any of these might legally be conditioned upon any decision of the pressured country. The pressure might not be effective, but there is no law against trying. Nonetheless, there are strong considerations relating to the development of an international order which bear both on the objectives sought and the means used.

In looking for criteria as to which pressures are appropriate and which are not, we may profit from the experience of individuals. When my neighbor asked my consent to build a carport nearer to our boundary than permitted by a building restriction, I conditioned my consent on his building a fence to hide the cars. As an alternative I might have conditioned my consent on his designating me as executor under his will. Although the first condition would cost him more money, it probably struck him as far more reasonable and less offensive than would have been the case with the second. The fence and the carport are directly and immediately related. Discussions between us were limited in scope to such things as the height, length, and type of fence. If I had suggested a price that had no relationship to the action sought other than that it involved the same person, I would have opened up every issue between us for possible inclusion in the bargain. I would also have appeared arbitrary and unreasonable, and for this reason my condition would be less easy to accept.

Such personal analogies suggest a general criterion where one country is seeking to bring pressure on another: the more direct and immediate the relationship between the pressure adopted and the end sought the better. This is not an either/or standard, but rather a matter of degree. In international relations it is desirable that coercion be in a form which is obviously relevant to the end sought. The more apparent and immediate the relevance, the less disruptive the pressure. The degree of relevance may, to be sure, be subject to intuitive judgment rather than measurement, but the general proposition can be illustrated. Perhaps with study it can be refined. The United States, for example, might appear to have no legitimate interest in what color another government painted its public buildings. For the United States to threaten to embargo all goods to that country unless it painted its public buildings green would seem to be unwise, and a gross meddling in the affairs of another country. Also, it might well prove to be ineffective, since it is politically difficult for governments to yield to pressure of that kind. On the other hand, if the United States had a surplus of green paint and offered to supply free paint for the public buildings of the other government provided that it decided to paint them green, there could be no possible objection. The rightness or wrongness of the pressure relates neither to the ends nor to the

26

means but to the directness of the relationship between the two.

In any one transaction the United States has its immediate short-run objective of getting results and its long-run objective of fostering an orderly pattern for handling questions arising among nations. Relating the pressure used directly to the ends sought will on some occasions aid in the accomplishment of the immediate objective by lessening resistance on the part of the coerced government. If coercion is immediately connected with the result sought, it seems fairer, it usually involves fewer officials (who are often in one minor part of the government), and acceding may not require a broad governmental decision.

On most occasions, however, the way to get quick results may be to use all available pressure no matter how remote from or unrelated to the action sought. In these cases the short-run interest of getting results must be weighed against the long-run interest which, I suggest, is promoted by trying to deal with each problem in terms of what is directly relevant to that particular problem. In one sense, so long as the world consists of national units, every event occurring within a country can be attributed to the government and identified as national action. In this way, any action with respect to a nation can be considered as relevant to any other action with respect to the same nation. For example a starving child, whom American Quakers would like to help, and a Communist editorial writer who attacks "Wall Street Capitalists" may both be in China. The United States might thus say that so long

27

as "you" criticize "us" in that way "we" will not give "you" wheat. Conduct within each country is attributed to the country as a whole, and all issues between people in the two countries are thus deemed interrelated. It is in this respect that the cold war is truly like a war. All events are related to a single national contest of wills. A commercial aviation agreement with the Soviet Union becomes relevant to a dispute over the status of East Germany.[6]

A wiser way to handle international conflict is illustrated by President Kennedy's response to the 1962 expropriation of American-owned property in Brazil. Members of Congress had introduced legislation to cut off all economic assistance to nations in which American assets had been expropriated without compensation. President Kennedy, pointing out that the property had been taken by the governor of a province, said: "I can think of nothing more unwise than to attempt to pass a resolution at this time which puts us in a position not of disagreement with a governor of a state who is not particularly our friend, but instead, really, with the whole Brazilian nation. . . ."[7]

In domestic law we have learned that it is useful to try to settle disputes on their merits rather than on an *ad hominem* basis. It may be useful to try to cope with international problems on their merits rather than on an *ad nationem* basis. Overall leverage may be appropriate in cases where one country is truly interested in the overall conduct of another country, as a psychiatrist is interested in the whole man. Where foreign aid is given because one country is interested in the economic development of another, the leverage need not be limited to the disposition of the particular products bought with the aid given. But as we have seen in the case of the proposal to deny welfare funds to mothers of illegitimate children, leverage is likely to be deemed harsh and will probably be unsuccessful unless its relevance to the conduct is apparent. Cutting off all economic aid to Laos as a means of putting pressure on the right-wing government to enter talks to form a coalition government encountered an initial reaction of defiance.[8]

Although there appears now to be no international law requiring non-forceful coercion to be reasonably related to the ends sought, international law does recognize that a country's absolute right to deny a benefit does not include the right to restrict it arbitrarily. A country may exclude all aliens if it wishes, but if it grants them permission to come in it must treat them according to certain minimum standards. In considering the development of the international law of peaceful coercion such precedents may be more relevant than those of forceful intervention which have been used in the past to support charges of "economic aggression."

These three problems in the field of intervention involve a great deal of policy and some international law. We international lawyers who seek a community governed by law must be prepared as part of our task to persuade governments to take steps in that direction. Most of such steps, from the point of view of a government official, depend on questions of policy, not of law. In arguing policy, however, we should not limit ourselves to the policy issues as they are seen by others. We must also try to present, in persuasive fashion, the arguments in favor of that all-important policy, the policy of resolving international questions according to principle and according to law.

1. See, *e.g.*, STOWELL, INTERVENTION IN INTERNATIONAL LAW (1921), HYDE, INTERVENTION IN THEORY AND PRACTICE, 9-10 (1911).

2. NY Times, April 23, 1961, p. 25.

3. The New York Times, for example, referred to "the Communist propaganda line already being dinned that the Americans have simply taken the place of the French rulers of Vietnam" (April 1, 1962, § 4, p. 5).

4. NY Times, February 25, 1962, p. 17.

5. *Id.*, April 1, 1962, § 4, p. 5.

6. *Id.*, August 22, 1962, p. 1.

7. *Id.*, March 8, 1962, p. 14.

8. *Id.*, March 6, 1962, p. 30.

The Legitimacy of Legislative
Intervention by the United Nations[1]

Richard A. Falk*

THE GROWTH of legal order is but one aspect of the on-
going experience of human civilization. As Erich
Kahler has said, "[T]he historical process entails a
gradual shift to broader units, and at the same time to
higher levels of consciousness."[2] This essay looks at
this process as it pertains to the gradual shift of authority and power from the nation to the United Nations. Not only is there an emergence of a broader
unit, but, as well, a higher level of consciousness. For
today we begin to perceive our self-interest as more
dependent upon the welfare of mankind than upon the
success of any particular nationality.

But old habits of loyalty and traditional residences of
power give way unwillingly to new wider claims. The
defenders of the nation remain ardent and numerous,

* Associate Professor of International Law, Woodrow Wilson
School of Public and International Affairs, and Research Associate,
Center of International Studies, Princeton University.

possess power, wield authority, and quickly solicit the enthusiasm of newly independent peoples. These defenders imperil the survival of man and his achievements of mind and spirit in an age when nuclear war threatens havoc and catastrophe. It remains doubtful whether the world can be transformed to a safer level of organization before it destroys itself in the course of this painful process of transition.

I

The traditional international order rested upon the primacy of the nation. Basic doctrines of sovereignty, territorial jurisdiction, equality of states, independence, nonintervention, and recognition each acknowledge this primacy. Yet it is a truism of the age that the nation no longer provides an adequate ordering unit for international relations. There is an urgent need for wider structures of authority supported by broader myths. This need informs our inquiry into the role of the United Nations in the life of domestic communities.

The orthodox view of the United Nations restricts its active role as a coercive agent to situations of violence which threaten or breach international peace. The presence of the United Nations in the Congo suggests, as did the earlier presence in Lebanon, that the distinctions between domestic and international violence and between pre-violence and violence are often impossible to make. It is clear that outbreaks or risks of internal violence increase the prospects of international warfare and can be treated as appropriate occasions for United Nations intervention. The insularity of the bloody language riots in India in the years following its independence contrast with the radiating impacts of civil strife in the Congo after its period of independence. There is no longer serious doubt about the Charter competence or the organizational willingness of the United Nations to protect the interest of the world in restraining radiating impacts of a serious internal war.

But international peace is not only threatened by internal warfare. Peace is also endangered by certain repressive social policies which, if allowed to remain unaltered, will produce serious outbreaks of domestic violence. This prospect prompts the central contention of this essay—that the United Nations should be authorized on a selective basis to coerce domestic social changes. This authorization is what we refer to throughout as legislative intervention. Actually this is a narrow competence although it is somewhat incompatible with many popular conceptions of the proper limits for United Nations action. Nevertheless, we argue that a limited legislative use of the United Nations finds its basis in the Charter as it has been interpreted and applied on prior occasions. Legislative intervention is nothing more than an extension of practice, an extension that has become imperative as a result of the delicate balance of forces that now keeps peace between the major states in the world. One achieves some sense of perspective about legislative intervention by the United Nations if one examines first the subject of intervention in general.

Intervention in internal affairs is a prominent characteristic of contemporary international conflict. On a single day a newspaper reports a new military buildup on American territory of Castro exiles planning a second invasion of Cuba and the construction of a supply road into Laos by Peking China to support the revolutionary cause of Pathet Lao.[3] At the same time, internal war rages in South Vietnam, initiated by a series of rather clandestine North Vietnamese guerrilla interventions and countered by strident American military intervention in apparent violation of the 1954 Geneva Accords.[4] Interventionary policy accounts for the most intense forms of violent conflict present in the world today.

The point is not to condemn these interventions, but to suggest that a foreign policy that depends upon unilateral military intervention by one nation in the affairs of another usually violates clear norms of international law, especially in the Western Hemisphere, where the standard of nonintervention has been worked out in a sequence of international agreements—solemnized as valid treaties. The willingness of the United States to adopt illegal interventionary tactics, under the pressure of the cold war, jeopardizes our moral commitment to a foreign policy of law-abidance, a commitment abstractly reiterated by our statesmen from many rostrums. More serious even than this hypocrisy is the fact that the stability of world politics requires the evolution of a reliable international legal order. This goal cannot be reached without the leadership of non-revolutionary societies, especially the

34

United States. For only a demonstration of the reality of a lawful alternative to power politics could tempt revolutionary nations to the point where they, too, might begin to perceive that the advantages of stability in a nuclear age outweigh the opportunities for expansion in an unstable world. For minimum order and security depend finally upon the joint willingness of all nuclear powers to establish a regime that is entrusted with the institutional management of force in world affairs; we need such a regime to overcome the dangers that arise from an obsolete reliance upon the tension between force and counter-force, the system of unstable equilibrium that continues to operate as the dominant ordering instrument of world politics.

Legislative intervention as a legitimate exercise of community power is intended to serve as a partial substitute for national intervention. The idea is to get certain domestic problems solved by the United Nations before they provoke domestic violence, the occasion that now so often induces rival national interventions. If we can eliminate the occasions upon which nations find it advantageous to use force—as by various interventions and indirect aggressions[5]—then the balance begins to tilt more heavily in favor of doing what must be done to cut the risks of nuclear war. Already the dangers of war discourage most recourse to direct aggression. The strength of the community mobilizes to resist expansion across international frontiers by armed attack. No nation, no matter how aggressive its objectives, can today adopt international war as a rational policy to achieve expansion. In complementary

35

fashion, legislative intervention by the United Nations seeks to undermine the rationality of striving for national or ideological expansion through intervention in the internal affairs of foreign states.

This proposal may seem to involve some qualification of traditional notions of sovereignty. For the world community acting through the United Nations is accorded certain over-seeing competences that appear to contradict the autonomy of the domestic order. But in fact, the domestic order has never enjoyed autonomy in any strict sense. It is now commonplace to accept the interdependence of economic, cultural, and military affairs. In fact, nations have always had a vital concern with what goes on elsewhere, even if elsewhere is a foreign state. Sovereignty only confers a primary competence upon a nation; it is not, and never was, an exclusive competence. Intervention in some form is an unavoidable concomitant of national existence. Pasquale Fiore's ideal international legal order acknowledged extra-national concern and competence by coupling a *duty* of collective intervention with a *duty* of nonintervention.[6] Similarly, when the United States renounced its interventionary claims which had grown so enormous in the afterglow of the Monroe Doctrine, it properly insisted that Latin America accept collective responsibilities for certain threatening domestic events in the hemisphere. The renunciation of intervention does not substitute a policy of nonintervention; it involves the development of some form of collective intervention. This is not, however, a Hobson's choice, for the degree of effective centralization achieved by a legal order with respect to coercion is a decisive criterion of its quality as law. Up to a certain point, it is not only centralization but the level and quality of institutionalization that gives the appearance of just law to action undertaken on behalf of the affected community. A contrast between the *ad hoc* collective interventions of the Holy Alliance and the collective interventions of a juridicial entity, like the Organization of American States, illustrates the relevance of institutionalization. Legislative intervention aims to combine the virtues of centralization with those of institutionalization.

Despite the confusion arising from the vagueness and multi-variant reference of "intervention," its use as a term remains worthwhile to throw light upon the effort of international law to allocate authority and power among units acting in international affairs; as we have said, the doctrine of nonintervention exists alongside notions of sovereignty, equality of states, territorial supremacy, self-determination, and rights of independence as a fundamental conception in the traditional system of international law. In a classical context, "nonintervention" expressed the duty that is correlative to the right to administer people, things, and events within national boundaries. This use of the term aptly calls attention to the norms of reciprocity that regulate a decentralized international order. In particular it reminds us that the principal actors are nations who are supposed to respect one another's sovereignty. However, "intervention" was not only used to describe self-serving interference; it also referred to action taken by one state to compel another state to maintain internal order or to satisfy international obligations. Diplomatic protection of aliens abroad led to extensive interventionary practice designed to uphold the legal rights of the nationals of the intervening power. In this way intervention could be made to serve as a sanction; intervention, so conceived, illustrated the dependence of law in a primitive community upon various techniques of self-help. Much of the bewilderment that accompanied notions of intervention arises from this contradictory heritage. For intervention was used both to allege a wrongful intrusion of one state into the affairs of another and to defend a sanctioning enterprise that was conducted by one state on behalf of the general community interest in law enforcement.[7] This helps to account for the curious fact that writers on international law appear to disagree as to whether intervention is legal or illegal.[8]

The legal status of intervention reflects the character of the prevailing international system. The arbitrariness of self-justifying intervention was challenged by smaller nations who demanded an increased adherence to the principles of sovereign equality. The success of this challenge is disclosed by the fact that no one seriously contends today that intervention by one nation in the affairs of another is authorized, as such, by the international legal order.[9] However, as the alternative to intervention is not nonintervention, but some form of collective intervention,[10] our inquiry is not at an end. In fact, it is about to begin. A contemporary appraisal of intervention must take into account the appropriate role in world affairs of a variety of non-national actors who increasingly exercise significant authority and power.

We are becoming familiar with the trans-national importance of the United Nations, the Organization of American States, the Soviet bloc, the Communist party, Radio Free Europe, the World Bank, the European Economic Community. These actors participate in world affairs in many ways, influencing especially the transformation of international law to meet the needs of the modern world. The activities of these non-national actors alter the context within which classical notions of intervention and nonintervention evolved. It is essential to reformulate the relations between national community and world with due regard to these altered conditions. It is in this spirit that it seems useful to explore the implications of entrusting the United Nations with a limited right of legislative intervention. It is, of course, essential to appreciate that the facts of interdependence contradict the possibility, as well as the aspiration or the allegation of duty, of adherence to a policy of absolute nonintervention. The power to intervene, whether used or not, is what influences domestic outcomes in another state in an "interventionary" manner. The choice, then, concerns the *form* of intervention. Paradoxically enough, "nonintervention" is one form of intervention.

The relative legitimacy of an intervention, as active intrusion in domestic affairs of a foreign state (as opposed to passive intrusion—"nonintervention"), is partly determined by the nature of the intervening actor. The quality of law is enhanced by centralizing decisions involving the application of coercion. This gives value to widening the political basis of intervention beyond national boundaries to take account of regional and world-wide attitudes and institutions. This preference for authorization, on as broad a basis as possible, does not deny that a given interventionary policy, no matter how collectivized by the relevant community, may on occasion abuse in an arbitrary manner the target state. Improved procedures for the official application of coercion can reduce, but not eliminate, injustice. In criminal trials, for instance, rules of evidence and due process cut the risks of unjust conviction. It is no argument against prevailing methods of handling the prosecution of crime to establish the occasional conviction of an innocent man. In realms of contingency, we strive for the most beneficial alternative among several imperfect ones.

It may sharpen this perspective of choice to describe several prominent types of intervention. First, there is the classical form of unilateral intervention by which one nation intervenes in the internal affairs of another. The Soviet intervention in Hungary in 1956 is illustrative, as is the bulk of United States practice under the Monroe Doctrine. Second, there is counter-intervention as when state A intervenes in the affairs of B to preempt or offset interference by state C. The present United States interventions in Laos and South Vietnam are justified as protection against imminent and actual Communist interventions. Third, there is collective intervention as when a number of states join to coerce the will of the target state. The intervention in 1827 by France, England, and Russia on behalf of the Greek insurgency against Turkish rule is an instance of this. Fourth, there is regional intervention as when a group of states forms a juridicial entity which then imposes the regional will upon a dissenting member of the group. The recent action of the Organization of American States against Cuba is an obvious illustration, but the interventions in the nineteenth century by the Holy Alliance on behalf of dynastic legitimacy also fit, although more dubiously, into this category. And fifth, there is universal intervention under the aegis of the United Nations. The Congo operation presents, perhaps, the clearest instance that we presently possess of this type of intervention.

My presentation asserts that each of these five types of intervention generates its own distinctive structure of normative restraint and tolerance. There is no single set of legal rules that is properly applicable to all interventionary phenomena. My central argument is based, in fact, upon the relative legality of United Nations interventions to achieve results that would be illegal if sought by unilateral or national interventions. In this respect one can locate the Soviet intervention of 1956 in Hungary, the O.A.S. intervention of 1962 in Cuba, and the U.N. intervention of 1960 in the Congo along a spectrum of ascending legality. However, it should be understood that the generality of the actor's base of authority is not the only determinant of legitimacy. For legitimacy also depends upon whether the intervention is based on prior principles

41

that express patterns of general community consent or merely reflect an *ad hoc* political majority of the moment. In this sense the earlier declarations of Caracas (1954) and San José (1960) alleging the incompatibility of communism with hemispheric values make the action taken at Punte del Este in 1961 appear less arbitrary. However, it is true that the dominance and insistence of the United States at the conference undermines, to some extent, the reality of community judgment. This tends to make the intervention look like a disguised version of the earlier practices of paternalistic intervention that the United States undertook throughout Latin America.

A definition of intervention may add some clarity to the discussion. With a full awareness of the difficulties of borderline application and the vagueness of the central variables, I offer the following definition of intervention: *"Intervention" refers to conduct with an external animus that intends to achieve a fundamental alteration of the state of affairs in the target nation.* Although any international actor may initiate intervention, only a state may be the victim of it. As William Burke shows well in his excellent treatment of minor coercion,[11] it is important to distinguish between the facts alleged to constitute intervention and the legal determination of these facts as intervention. Does a documented assertion that United States military aid to South Vietnam constitutes "intervention" make it "intervention" in a legal sense? This kind of question illustrates the importance of identifying the decision-makers authorized to interpret and apply the norms of intervention. This is a critical inquiry for any legal order, but it is especially so in the international legal order. The decentralized character of international relations often makes the authoritative decision-maker hard to locate, if not actually indeterminate.[12] For instance, in view of the United Nations rejection of Cuba's competence to complain in any higher forum about the illegality of the sanctions voted at Punta del Este, how can we assess the legality of the O.A.S. action? Such a line of analysis, if pursued insistently, tends to identify "law" with the decisions of those entitled by the legal system to render them, and refers always to a "higher" authority capable of appraising the contested decision.[13]

II

Sir Frederick Maitland describes the rise of the Court of Chancery of fourteenth-century England as "an exceedingly curious episode." He observes that "the whole nation seems to enter into one large conspiracy to evade laws which it has not the courage to reform. The Chancellor, the Judges, and the Parliament seem all to be in the conspiracy." But as Sir Frederick goes on so shrewdly to observe, this was not really a conspiracy at all, but a gradual and sublimal transformation of the legal order on a case-to-case basis by honest men intent on justice in a series of particular controversies that happened to come before the Chancellor. Maitland also suggests that "somehow or other England, after a fashion all her own, had stumbled into a scheme for the reconciliation of permanence with progress."[14] It seems, of course, that this example strays rather perversely from my topic, but I refer to Maitland's account of the rise of equity jurisprudence in order to highlight the problems of peaceful change that exist for *any* legal order, even though my interest is in the problem of peaceful change only as it exists for the international order. The more crafty purpose of using this analogy is to invoke the dignity of Maitland and the conservatism of England to soften a hostile response to what may sound, at first, like a heretical solution for the problem of peaceful change in the international environment.

The crux of the problem can be put as a familiar question: How can we reconcile permanence with progress in international affairs? [15] The acuteness of the crisis that prompts the question is a rapid obsolescence of the traditional mechanism for change (war) and the absence of an adequate institution entrusted with responsibility for change (legislature). It is in this setting that I urge consideration of my proposal to endow the United Nations with a restricted legislative competence to intervene in domestic affairs. This competence would authorize United Nations intervention whenever civil strife threatens world peace or whenever gross abuses of fundamental human rights take place. It should be stressed that formal authorization is different from a set of recommendations. Authorization is concerned with the empowering of the United Nations to act, not with action itself. Prudential considerations of feasibility may often preclude the pursuit of an interventionary policy otherwise authorized. Thus, for instance, the power of the Soviet Union properly inhibited United Nations participation in the 1956 internal wars of Eastern Europe. Dangers of military escalation make it imperative that any advocacy of a policy of coercion appraise impacts upon the state of equilibrium within the entire international system, as well as the probable impacts upon the subsystem within which action is taken. It is crucial here to keep in mind the standard-setting, precedent-establishing quality of conduct in a social order in which power is broadly distributed; reciprocal adherence to standards and judicious self-restraint, rather than police precedures, are the principal ordering devices. Thus, for instance, a United States decision to share nuclear weapons technology authorizes symmetrical conduct by the Soviet Union.

An argument for legislative intervention is radical, at least on its surface, as it proposes that organs of the United Nations extend their competence from intersocietal conflict to embrace, as well, certain specified occasions of non-violent intra-societal conflict. Such a position appears to run contrary to ideas of national sovereignty and domestic jurisdiction that many observers regard as the firm basis of the United Nations. It is, of course, true that the Charter asserts that the United Nations "is based on the principle of sovereign equality" (Article 2[1]) and that "nothing contained in the present Charter shall authorize the United Nations to intervene in matters which are essentially within the domestic jurisdiction of any state" (Article 2[7]).

Despite these norms of deference to national societies, it seems clear that the Charter includes contrary assumptions of community responsibility that are sufficient to meet the needs of a developing international order. My argument for legislative competence accords precedence to the successful discharge of the affirmative responsibilities given by member nations to the United Nations. In this connection, it is important to regard the Charter as the organic law of a primitive world community. Perhaps it is helpful to imitate the imaginative response of John Marshall to the United States Constitution during its period of early development. Such a response engenders an attitude that perceives law not as a fixed matrix, but as a dynamic dimension of social change. The international order presently needs to use law in this flexible way if it is to adapt the old system to the new demands.

This gives an orientation. For the legislative use of the United Nations is an aspect of the larger problem of facilitating changes in the international system in a manner that transforms rather than destroys the prevailing standards of order. The aspirations of the modernizing nations in Africa, Asia, and Latin America and the revolutionary nations belonging to the Sino-Soviet bloc challenge deeply the authority of the traditional system of international law as it was developed by a few powerful Christian states of Western Europe who preached capitalist ethics and practiced imperialism. On a political level this challenge fans the flames of domestic discord throughout the world, giving grievance groups strong external backing. Cold war rivalry generates patterns of intervention and counter-intervention to offset attempts by the ideological enemy to extend its sphere of political influence. The result is a familiar series of costly internal wars, divided national polities, and recurrent crises in the international relations of the nuclear superstates. The presence of nuclear weapons does give all states some incentive, although a variable one, to find a way to achieve fundamental domestic transitions by peaceful means, or failing this, by the minimum use of violence. This incentive appears to support co-operative action on a supranational level, at least with respect to those social changes that generate a strong consensus among the states. The possibilities for political integration in today's world depend as much upon the discernment of consensus as upon the resolution of conflict.

Efforts to encourage the hermetic solution of domestic conflict will not assure adequate outcomes, even assuming, as is doubtful, the capacity to seal off domestic politics from external intrusions. For one thing, reactionary elites, with an apparatus of repression at their disposal, can often deny progressive movements opportunities to reach their goals by peaceful or constitutional means. This provides protest groups with a choice between an abandonment of the protest and resort to extra-legal means, usually involving violence. Fundamental social reorderings of power rarely take place, except perhaps in highly industrialized societies with long democratic traditions, without a period of sustained insurgency and rebellion, often culminating in bitter civil strife. Oppressive regimes can usually frustrate the objectives of domestic rebellion even when the rebels have the overwhelming support of the population. To counteract this insurgent groups solicit intervention from sympathetic external sources. In current world politics this tends to draw an internal war into the midst of the cold war, especially if the domestic arena of conflict is an uncommitted nation.[16] Of course, this process is abetted by the sense of revolutionary mission within the Sino-Soviet bloc. This combination of domestic frustration and revolutionary ideology produces an atmosphere that is very conducive to intervention. Cold war rivalry, however, encourages counter-intervention and preventive intervention. Intervention and counter-intervention increase the magnitude and intensity of internal conflict, yet often yield an indecisive outcome, leaving the basis for unrest present in the post–internal–war society. Frequently, to prevent escalation, the opposing interveners agree upon a stalemate, imposing the solution upon the domestic society which is the actual arena of violence. The internal wars of Asia that have led to the interventionary participation of rival cold war blocs in the years since World War II adhere to this pattern with intimidating fidelity. It is urged that we consider the feasibility of United Nations intervention as a beneficial alternative to the destructive and indecisive quality of symmetrical intervention by nuclear rivals. One can assert the preliminary legitimacy of United Nations intervention merely by suggesting the very obvious threat to international peace that exists whenever nuclear nations invest their prestige and power in the outcome of an internal war. Wherever action is necessary to eliminate such risks, the United Nations seems authorized, if not obliged, to take action.

However, there is a broader base upon which to rest United Nations intervention. For wherever the objectives of domestic insurgency express fundamental preferences of the world community, then the outcome of internal war automatically becomes a matter of international concern. To reach the 1962 Evian Accords the Algerian War, fulfilling the anti-colonial will of the Moslem plurality of 9:1, required 250,000 lives and $20,000,000,000.[17] And yet such an outcome, despite the persistence of extremist terror, appears to have been inevitable from the outset. Thus it would appear beneficial to have used the co-ordinated power of the world community to achieve the inevitable outcome with greater decisiveness and less bloodshed. Of course, enormous problems of technique arise whenever political rivals embark on a co-operative venture. Often the common basis for action dissolves, replaced by antagonistic views of the appropriate way to structure the outcome. Nevertheless, the costs of restraint appear higher in many instances. The Congo operation suggests the benefits and dangers of relying upon an apparent community consensus to manage the outcome of domestic strife.

Despite the difficulties of sustaining an initial consensus, it seems advantageous to increase United Nations responsibility for speeding certain processes of social change. The benefit is to find short cuts to social progress that enhance the dignity of mankind and avoid the necessity to rely upon a prolonged transition marked by costly violence. The domestic situations in Angola and South Africa will predictably generate widespread violence to overcome colonial domination and institutional racism. Both violent protest movements will reach their objectives. But there exists an area of creative adaptation that presents a range of choices which point the way toward the outcome, and, hence, control the quality of the outcome itself. There are all sorts of ways to end colonial domination with more or less benefit to the domestic community and to the stability of world order. Why should the world community, almost universally opposed to colonialism and racism, remain an aloof spectator while the process of tension, conflict, and violent resolution works itself out? The repudiation of the incumbent policies is not just a matter of domestic protest; it is an expression of the overwhelming consensus that exists in the international community. The oppressed domestic groups assert their claims as a result of an awareness of their situation and its alternatives that almost always comes from contact with ideas and situations that exist outside the domestic order. Internal wars are deeply embedded in supranational social and political processes. The alternative to United Nations intervention is likely to be a cold war settlement of internal strife. This raises the risks of escalation and increases the costs of human suffering to intolerable levels.

50

For these reasons this essay supports United Nations intervention as a legislative act of the world community, seeking, principally, to promote world stability and fundamental human rights. Practice already discloses this legislative competence. The participation of the United Nations in the Congo is an assertion of world community insistence upon internal order in circumstances threatening world peace, even though processes of self-determination are sacrificed. United Nations resolutions of censure condemning Portugal's administration of Angola express world community support for insurgent objectives, even though notions of domestic legitimacy are thereby undercut. Discussions and condemnations of the treatment of non-whites in the Republic of South Africa express the opposition of the world community to political structures of racial domination, even though the territorial supremacy of the incumbent regime is thereby challenged. In general, world community policies in these areas are already given precedence over traditional deferences to national sovereignty. Anti-colonialism and anti-racism are becoming legislative norms governing United Nations conduct. This assumption of competence on the part of the organization has not been seriously questioned in recent practices of the United Nations (except, of course, by the targets or victims and their friends). Controversy and formidable obstacles arise whenever implementation of this legislative competence uncovers cold war rivalry. In general, Western democracies advocate persuasive interference while revolutionary and ex-colonial nations prefer coercive interference, but each assumes the legitimacy of interference. Thus the legitimacy of United Nations legislative intervention seems increasingly established by the overwhelming support of member nations for a series of *ad hoc* ventures. We recall the relevance of Maitland's account of the rise of equity to suggest that there might appear to be a conspiracy by the membership of the United Nations to violate its own restraining norms. But here, too, it is only an apparent conspiracy arising from a case-to-case response by the organization to the desperate need of the world community to stabilize serious threats to nuclear peace and the presence of a vital consensus to carry out the Charter mandate to promote fundamental human rights. That is, legislative competence results from a series of gradual accretions which begin to form new standards of legitimacy. This process of agglutinative reform gives flexibility to what would otherwise become a rigid regime governed by an outmoded organic law.

Even from a strictly juridical perspective the basis for expanding United Nations participation in domestic affairs seems quite convincing. For the domestic jurisdiction exception is made explicitly subject to the overriding responsibility of the United Nations to maintain peace. The cold war and the development of nuclear weapons and electronic guidance systems make it necessary to anticipate threats to the peace at a stage prior to resort to international violence. Internal wars and obsolete domestic repressions are two political contexts in which it is quite possible to initiate an escalation cycle that ends in nuclear war.

Thus the present condition of unstable equilibrium between nuclear antagonists links the advocacy of United Nations intervention to the maintenance of peace between nations. This provides the interpretative basis for construing the limitations imposed on the United Nations by Article 2(7). Crucial phrases like "to intervene in matters," "essentially within," and "domestic jurisdiction" acquire the gloss imposed by these altered minimum prerequisites of world peace.

Two important qualifications must now be mentioned. First, and this is too complicated to do more than acknowledge, advocacy of U.N. intervention is accompanied by serious reservations about the role and reliability of the United Nations as a lawmaking and law-applying institution. My position is simply that U.N. legislative intervention is the best available alternative to serve the community interests of the world in a time when national rivals stand poised to destroy one another (and a lot of others) in a nuclear war. It is not very good, but it is better than anything else that we have—better by far than continuing to tolerate internal wars fought as proxy wars between intervening nuclear powers.

The second qualification of my thesis arises from the special character of the United Nations as a political institution. The United Nations possesses scant autonomous power. Its decisions require the backing of its members, and especially the support of the powerful states. Effective action cannot be taken against a superpower except, perhaps, if it clearly violates the prime norm of the contemporary legal system by making a significant armed attack across a national boundary. Thus legislative intervention requires a consensus within the organization that transcends the fissures of the cold war. We find such a consensus operative with respect to the initial authorization of the Congo operation and with regard to the existing situation in Angola and South Africa. It is essential that the United Nations achieve the status of a community organization, and resist the inclination to become a political weapon in the cold war. The United States, especially in the early years of the United Nations, with easy majorities at its disposal, used the organization rather irresponsibly to act as a holy alliance against the Soviet bloc. The treatment of the China issue, especially the retention of Formosa on the Security Council, continues, it is felt, to underrate the national value to the United States of having the United Nations achieve the identity of a world community, acting to fulfill universal interests to the extent that they exist, however limited they may now appear to be.[18]

The appropriate institution for partisan supranational action is to be found on the regional level. Here the stabilizing value of political homogeneity for a group of closely related states favors a political use of regional organizations even though this may involve, on occasion, a betrayal of the ideal of national self-determination. It is the rationale of solidarity that seems most strongly to support the 1962 action taken against Castro's Cuba at Punta del Este which resulted in the exclusion of the present Cuban government from the inter-American system on the ground that adherence to Marxism-Leninism was incompatible with the politics of the hemisphere. In effect, the Soviet suppressions of the uprisings in East Germany, Poland, and Hungary similarly, although more brutally, expressed a *regional* intolerance of the principle of peaceful coexistence. It is unfortunate in many respects to compel dissenting national communities to conform to regional political preferences, but it may be indispensable for the maintenance of minimum conditions of international stability. As such, a reciprocal tolerance implicitly develops to accept intra-bloc interventions, especially if authorized by a regional organization, to prevent a fundamental defection from existing bloc affiliation.[19] This rule of the game—in effect, a norm acknowledging spheres of influence—does not presently apply to non-aligned nations *inter sese*, although it is quite possible that adherence to the politics of non-alignment may also emerge soon as a regulative norm for this increasingly important group of nations.[20]

This discussion of regional intervention intends to reinforce the significance of coexistence within the United Nations, especially with respect to legislative activity. The decentralized distribution of power, nuclear bipolarity, diversity of social and economic philosophy restrict effective coercion by the United Nations to areas within which there exists an almost universal consensus, and certainly agreement about basic legislative objectives on the part of the major cold war rivals. From this perspective even the Soviet

55

championship of the troika principle seems less irresponsible. However, the reasonableness of troika-type restraint if applied to areas of legislative policy would become unreasonable if principles applicable to internal violence are extended to occasions of actual or threatened international violence. For the United Nations cannot permit itself to allow the cold war to take precedence over the need to mobilize community resources against potential violators of the international peace. The non-aligned nations deserve considerable credit for their resistance to troika, as it required them to subordinate their belief in coexistence and active neutralism to the demands for a non-political response to situations involving force.

Internal wars often present intermediate situations partly calling forth rules of limitation appropriate to the role of the United Nations in the light of the cold war and partly counseling the unified intervention of the world community. In general, if the conflict can be internationalized prior to cold war involvement, then the United Nations can act effectively to stabilize the domestic society and keep the cold war out of the civil conflict. If cold war interventions already have significantly taken place, then the United Nations cannot restore order without choosing sides; a consequence of such a choice is to antagonize deeply the nations supporting the faction repressed by the United Nations. The Congo operation became problematic partly because the non–cold war domestic conflict acquired a cold war quality in the course of United Nations intervention. However, entry by the United

Nations at a pre–cold war phase solicited wide community support for a Congo settlement as an alternative to unrestricted internal war. One contrasts the situation in the Congo with the possible control by the United Nations of the internal wars presently raging in Laos and South Vietnam. U.N. intervention in these internal wars would need to stabilize the domestic scene by giving exclusive governmental authority to a single elite. This would require a choice between the warring elites, thus allying the United Nations with one cold war bloc against the other in a conflict situation that has been already fully articulated on the level of international ideological rivalry.

If U.N. intervention is requested by the legitimately constituted government prior to a state of full-fledged insurgency, then there is some reason to argue in behalf of a community response. This was the situation in Lebanon in 1958, where United Nations presence was a compromise alternative to American military intervention to bolster the shaky Chamoun regime. Here, as with the Congo, the United Nations was able to stabilize a threatening domestic situation, even when it was a part of the cold war, because it entered before the threshold of violence had been decisively crossed.

Coercive forms of intervention by the United Nations against a legitimate government, given the continuing strength of the principle of nationalism and the comparative weakness of the Organization, depend on the formation of a consensus that unites the superpowers in the pursuit of common interventionary goals. The advantages of overcoming colonialism or racism by world community standards and pressures, rather than by protracted civil war, commend the adoption of a more radical approach to legislative intervention by the United Nations. This would appear to be a stabilizing way to compel constituted governments to abandon their insistence upon adhering to highly objectionable policies and practices. An expanding competence for legislative intervention would help to create the kind of political stability that might eventually induce revolutionary nations to renounce recourse to indirect aggression and subversion. The attainment of such stability is also an essential aspect of the quest to create a social and political climate that is favorable for disarmament negotiations. As such, it expresses our responsibility to use all available means to achieve the urgent, but hazardous, transition to a warless world. The argument for legislative intervention presupposes that the activity of the United Nations will be designed to promote the values that we proclaim, requiring some acceleration of normal processes of social change in domestic societies, but change that is almost inevitable in the light of certain overwhelming historical pressures, as those that mount against colonialism or institutional racism.

This essay concludes with another reference to Maitland's analysis of equity jurisprudence. In his masterful summing up Maitland reports that although the legal innovations of the Star Chamber and Chancery Court *were* severe threats to the political liberties of Englishmen, nevertheless, "if we look abroad [to Continental Europe] we shall find good reason for thinking that but for these institutions our old-fashioned national law, unable out of its own resources to meet the requirements of the new age, would have utterly broken down, and the 'ungodly jumble' would have made way for Roman jurisprudence and despotism." [21] So it may be that historians looking back on the second half of the twentieth century will conclude that but for the ungodly jumble of legislative intervention by the United Nations the traditional system of international law and order would have been buried in oblivion far beneath the ruins wrought by some great nuclear conflagration.

1. I am glad to acknowledge the influence that Professor Saul H. Mendlovitz of the Rutgers Law School has had upon this essay. We have collaborated on an article dealing with many of these issues that is scheduled to appear in the Yale Law Journal early in 1964 with the title *Towards a Warless World: One Legal Formula to Achieve Transition.*
I would also like to call attention to an excellent paper that expresses a kindred approach to the link between intervention and social change: M. Halpern, "The Morality of American Intervention in the Internal Affairs of Other States" (mimeographed distribution by the Council on Religion and International Affairs), 1962.

2. Kahler, *Culture and Evolution,* 5 CENTENNIAL REVIEW, 239, 258 (1961).

3. NY Times, April 19, 1962, pp. 1, 5, 15.

4. The United States, although not a party to the Accords, did indicate its willingness to govern its behavior by the standards adopted in 1954 at Geneva. *Cf* legalistic rhetoric of Soviet attack on United States intervention in South Vietnam, N. Y. Times, March 18, 1962, p. 30.

5. If it is possible to discourage these residual uses of aggressive force in world politics, then the argument for

community management of force grows correspondingly stronger. For if it is imprudent to seek expansion by indirect use of force, by interventionary tactics, then the risks of nuclear war by miscalculation, accident, catalytic agent, and escalation assume apparent dominance. This, in turn, helps to converge the perspectives of national interest and international peace.

6. FIORE, INTERNATIONAL LAW CODIFIED AND ITS LEGAL SANCTION OR THE LEGAL ORGANIZATION OF THE SOCIETY OF STATES 265-72 (5th ed. Borchard transl. 1918).

7. See Fenwick, *Intervention: Individual and Collective,* 39 AM. J. INT'L L. 645 (1945).

8. The most sustained defense of the legality of intervention is provided by STOWELL, INTERVENTION IN INTERNATIONAL LAW (1921).

9. There is, however, a developing tolerance for symmetrical counter-intervention. That is, if A intervenes on behalf of faction X in state B, then C is entitled to intervene on behalf of faction Y to neutralize the effect of A's illegal intervention.

10. Of course, the distinction between unilateral and collective intervention over-generalizes for emphasis. The preference for collective intervention is an indication of emphasis. It does not purport to be a new standard of law.

11. See Burke, *The Legal Regulation of Minor International Coercion: A Framework of Inquiry, infra,* pp. 88-89.

12. It is the importance of this inquiry that makes study of the *Nottebohm* judgment so suggestive.

13. Domestic analogies are instructive. For instance, the United States has developed a theory of judicial review to vindicate its search for authoritative decisions on the issue of constitutionality, whereas Great Britain relies upon a theory of parliamentary supremacy to achieve a parallel result.

14. MAITLAND & MONTAGUE, A SKETCH OF ENGLISH LEGAL HISTORY 127 (1915). (Chapter V, "Growth of Statute and Common Law and Rise of the Court of Chancery, 1307-1600," written by Maitland.)

15. For good general inquiries see VISSCHER, THEORY AND REALITY IN PUBLIC INTERNATIONAL LAW 308-24 (Cor-

bett transl. 1957); RÖLING, INTERNATIONAL LAW IN AN EXPANDED WORLD (1960).

16. There is a tendency to remain aloof from a civil war that takes place in a society closely allied with either nuclear superpower. Thus the United States did not intervene in Hungary in 1956, nor did the Soviet Union intervene in Guatemala in 1954 nor in Cuba prior to the victory of Castro in 1959. The high risks of escalation evidently inhibit interventions in this set of instances. See generally Schwarzenberger, *Hegemonial Intervention,* THE YEAR BOOK OF WORLD AFFAIRS 236-65 (1955).

17. N.Y. Times, March 19, 1962, p. 13.

18. There is a need to give attention to the discernment of areas of global consensus and its implications for world order. This inquiry would complement concern with conflict resolution.

19. The refusal of the United Nations in 1961-62 to consider seriously Cuba's complaints about regional coercion provides interesting confirmation.

20. That is, non-aligned states may come to take interventionary measures to prevent a state from shifting its affiliation from neutralist identification to cold war partisanship.

21. MAITLAND & MONTAGUE, *op. cit. supra* note 14, at 127-28.

Intervention: Benefaction as Justification

Michael H. Cardozo[*]

IN HIS ARTICLE on non-intervention that appeared in
the Howard Law Journal in 1959, Richard Falk
analyzed the problem of defining "intervention" and
discussed the tendency of some commentators to enlarge the concept "almost indefinitely." [1] He referred
to the question raised by Professors McDougal and
Lasswell of whether the concept should be limited
exclusively to the threat of force or whether it may
also "catch the more subtle modalities of coercion." [2]
While not wanting to enlarge the concept "almost
indefinitely," I do want, in this paper, to consider the
permissibility of a kind of influence exerted by the
United States on other nations that, while certainly
not properly called "subtle," may also not be classified
as one of the "cruder, physical forms" of international

---

*Professor of Law and Director of International Legal Studies,
Cornell University.

coercion. I refer to the provision of generous amounts of economic, technical, and military "aid" to other nations over the past twenty years, under programs that have permitted the United States government to meddle in the affairs of other nations more intimately than would have been possible in an earlier era.

"Each such country shall conclude an agreement with the United States in order for such country to be eligible to receive assistance under this title." [3] Summed up in that clause of the Economic Cooperation Act of 1948, the authorizing legislation for the European Recovery Program, are all the attitudes that underlie the imposition of "conditions of aid" which have become so characteristic of the "foreign aid" programs of the United States.[4] The practice of exacting conditions has led us to ask for undertakings that permit us, in the words of Ernest A. Gross, then the legal adviser of the Department of State, to "burrow deep into the internal economy" of each participating country.[5] Such a "mechanism of donor control" has been characterized by Professor McDougal and Dr. Feliciano as coercion of one of the milder degrees of intensity, but they accept it nonetheless as a form of intervention.[6] Perhaps it is of so mild a degree as to avoid the proscription of the United Nations Charter. Still, it was sufficiently intense and novel in 1948 to lead Mr. Gross to point out that the Economic Cooperation Agreements of 1948 were "unique in the history of dealings between modern states." Whether the intervention should be considered permissible because of its voluntary acceptance, or impermissible

64

because of a lurking coercion, will be the subject of this paper.

The motives that have led the United States to intervene with "conditions of aid" are easy to understand. No matter how many semantic devices were used to avoid calling the aid programs a kind of benefaction, they were certain to be considered "foreign aid," and some skeptics would call them mere "giveaway programs." In the enacting clause of the Lend-Lease Act, the statute was called "An act to promote the defense of the United States,"[7] and Mr. Stettinius's book on lend-lease was subtitled *Weapon for Victory*.[8] Still, in the popular mind it was "aid to our allies." The Marshall Plan was officially named "The European Recovery Program," and the enabling statute, "The Economic Cooperation Act of 1948," was called "An Act to Promote World Peace and the General Welfare, National Interest and Foreign Policy of the United States."[9] Nevertheless, the idea that the participating countries were going to "receive assistance" from the United States was reflected even in various sections of the law, such as section 115 (b), quoted at the start of this paper.

This recurring divergence between the conception of these programs in the minds of their architects and the practical views of the elected politicians stems from fuzziness and vacillation in thinking about their essential purpose. Are we altruistically helping other needy nations, or are we selfishly or patriotically furthering the needs of our own foreign policy? As soon as a program looks to a viewer like a "world-wide

WPA," [10] or simply a compassionate measure to give aid to the less fortunate, it is quite normal for him to expect conditions binding the supplicant to put his house in order, politically as well as economically, and in our kind of order. We can tell him to forego evil companions, to do business with our traders, and even to respect the rights of men as required by our Constitution. To the man on the diplomatic front lines, however, it will be more obvious that the program's greatest virtue will be its contribution to the maintenance of "a world environment predominantly made up of open societies . . . in which our form of democratic society can persist and develop." [11] This is what we have at stake, in the view of those who first proposed such programs. To them, we are "promoting the general welfare and national defense" of the United States when we spend billions of dollars for economic recovery, technical development, and military strength in countries that are or may be on our side in a cold or a hot war. Perhaps it is true that only an idealistic people, with a tradition of neighborliness and humanitarianism, would think of helping themselves by helping others. There is always likely to be a bit of selfishness in acts of charity. The nature of our "foreign aid" programs, therefore, is probably a mixture of national interest and altruism. The extent to which conditions are justified may simply depend on which motive is predominant in the particular time and place.

Let us look at the kinds of conditions the United States has imposed, and their effectiveness, in connection with large-scale programs of financial support for other countries. A good point of departure is the refinancing of the debts of Germany after World War I, because none of the kinds of conditions applied after World War II can be found in the Dawes and Young Plans.[12] In those days such conditions imposed on an independent major nation, even a former enemy, would surely have evoked cries of improper intervention in domestic affairs. Memories of coercive measures against lesser, though equally independent, powers would have made most of the now familiar conditions wholly unacceptable. In the outcome, however, the purposes of the two Plans, and of a few billions of dollars of loans affected with governmental encouragement through private channels, were wholly frustrated by the failure of Germany and others to follow internal practices that the conditions of the later programs would have demanded. Wise counselors predicted the failure of the policies, but without avail.[13] This experience was fresh in the minds of American legislators when the exigencies of the logistics of World War II led to the adoption of the lend-lease program.

The Lend-Lease Act itself specifies practically no conditions to be imposed on the sharing of resources needed to win the war. It was proposed and adopted in the spirit that "the total fighting and productive power that each of the United Nations can put into our combined operations to defeat our common enemies is of benefit to all the others." [14] As the reports to Congress continually emphasized, lend-lease and reverse lend-lease were intended to "involve neither

67

gifts, nor loans or transfers of money. They are, instead, a system of mutual war supply." [15] The concept of "mutual benefit" was so strong and clear to most of the legislators that there could be no thought of restrictive conditions.

Not long after the act was passed, however, there began to appear the confusion of thought that has characterized such programs ever since. First came cries that the British were re-exporting scarce supplies taken from our hard-pressed economy (rationing here was soon to begin, comparable to measures the British had accepted two years before). These exports of goods "given without charge" were said to be maintaining or creating markets for British commerce that would compete with our producers. The British, of course, pointed to their all-embracing war effort as preventing any possibility of such transgressions. Still, it seemed important, before more funds should be sought for lend-lease "aid," to create a mechanism to provide assurance against leaks. Consequently, the British issued a White Paper containing firm commitments against the diversion of lend-lease materials from "the prosecution of the war effort" or to "the furtherance of private interests." [16] Assurances against re-export were given, and additional measures were promised to prevent unnecessary exports of "materials of a type the use of which is being restricted in the United States on the grounds of short supply" and which were entering the British Isles through lend-lease or otherwise. Additional clauses assured the control of profits in transactions in England involving lend-lease goods or similar materials. A special office in the Lend-Lease Administration was established to watch over the British economy to assure compliance with the White Paper and to be prepared at all times to reassure congressmen that the British were not feathering their nests through the products of the lend-lease appropriations. Averell Harriman headed the office in Washington before he became the chief lend-lease representative in London. Standing between the American congressmen clamoring for control of the always suspect British traders and the hard-pressed Englishmen who acutely felt the burdens placed on their countrymen by rationing, sinkings, and bombings, this was a most delicate mission. It was the prototype, however, of many others to follow during the next two decades.

The British White Paper was the most conspicuous example of conditions imposed on the continuance of lend-lease supplies. In a sense, of course, every special mission in a lend-lease country was charged with observing the uses of material supplied through the program. Their chief function, however, was to make recommendations on the needs of the country concerned. Sometimes, however, the lend-lease representative became the means of imposing conditions that would normally have been labeled improper intervention in domestic affairs. For example, suppose essential goods from the United States were going to a lend-lease country for distribution on the civilian market. Would the local representative of lend-lease recommend that export licenses be granted in the face of evidence that the goods were being allotted by local authorities in a manner that would discriminate against despised minorities? Suppose the discrimination was only against foreign firms, such as American subsidiaries and affiliates. This kind of problem arose in more than one country, and more than once the United States refused to be a party to the discrimination. Was it none of our business, or was it permissible intervention to use the mild coercion available because of the other nation's urgent need for the goods?

Some Americans, at least, thought we ought to take full advantage of the dire needs of our allies and obtain massive concessions in return for lend-lease aid. Several times on the floor of the Senate, for example, the call was made to obtain from the British grants of various territories in the Western Hemisphere for military bases and concessions for large quantities of various minerals in which we were deficient. We should demand all these "now, while the war is on," said the senators.[17] One senator said that he could not find out if lend-lease is a "one-way street . . . or whether we are receiving any value in return for what we send to our allies." [18] At the same moment those allies were huddled in air-raid shelters trying to escape the buzz bombs that our common enemies were sending them. The reaction of the senator was a far cry from that of President Roosevelt, who once said that "victory and a sure peace are the only coin in which we can be repaid" for what we sent under lend-lease.[19] He saw it as a pooling of resources by allies, not as a donation by a benefactor.

As the war came to a close, relief and rehabilitation

measures were organized under UNRRA, perhaps the first program of its kind to be operated by a multilateral organization. For purposes of this paper its significance lay in the impossibility of using UNRRA shipments as a means of exacting conditions with a nationalistic hue. UNRRA did impose conditions, such as the sequestration of funds realized from the sale of commodities.[20] But none of the conditions could further the aims of one country or one bloc. Although it was a very valuable program, and did an important job effectively, UNRRA was one of the most unpopular "aid" programs ever accepted by the U.S. Congress. The suspicion keeps arising that it was its immunity to our unilateral conditions that turned the congressmen against it.

The "aid" programs that followed UNRRA had certain built-in conditions that were to become standard parts of the legislation of the period. The two "relief" acts of 1947 called for the establishment of special missions in recipient countries to "have direct supervision and control . . . of relief supplies" furnished by the United States.[21] In the Greek-Turkish Assistance Act of 1947 each country had to agree "as a condition precedent to the receipt of any assistance" under the act, to let U.S. officials have "free access . . . for the purpose of observing whether such assistance is utilized effectively and in accordance with the undertakings" of the government concerned.[22] Among other conditions, the Greek and Turkish governments had to agree "to give full and continuous publicity within such country, as to the purpose, source, character, scope and amounts, and progress of United States economic assistance" provided under the act.[23] In reading these provisions, it is hard to remember that, in passing the law, Congress had recognized that "the national integrity and survival of these nations are of importance to the security of the United States and of all freedom-loving peoples . . . ."[24] Some of the conditions seem to place more emphasis on the next clause, that the national integrity and survival of these nations "depend upon the receipt at this time of assistance." It is clear that the avowed purposes of the act were mixed, but the true purpose was obscure. Surely, however, our real reason for embarking on the program was to support our effort to "contain" communism, an effort of the highest priority in our national policy at the time, supported by a bipartisanship that was more typical of wartime than peace. Of course, it was the opening of the cold war, and the Greek-Turkish program was one of the campaigns to win that war. Was the program, therefore, a proper vehicle on which we could properly base conditions? Would we have refused aid if one of the governments had been unwilling to agree to all the statutory conditions? Iran may be the only country whose leaders have actually told us we could take our aid and its conditions and go home. We were very distressed when the grouchy Mossadegh did this. Indonesia has also balked at some of our conditions. Since then, "aid" legislation generally has had "escape" clauses, permitting us to continue aid despite the refusal of a country to accept conditions that might turn out not to be "applicable" or "appropriate" under the circumstances.[25]

In the legislation for the European Recovery Pro-

72

gram there is found the most formidable list of conditions of all the various enactments. The American people were, in the words of Mr. Gross, "fed up with rat-hole relief."[26] The participating countries, which, it must be recalled, included most of the well-developed and anti-Communist nations of Western Europe, had to agree to support measures—[27]

1. To increase production of coal, steel, transportation facilities, and food.

2. To stabilize currency, establish or maintain a valid rate of exchange.

3. To balance their governmental budgets.

4. To restore or maintain confidence in their monetary systems.

5. To reduce barriers to trade among themselves and with other countries.

6. To make efficient and practical use of their resources for recovery, including locating and using assets in the United States belonging to their nationals.

7. To facilitate the transfer to the United States by sale, barter, or otherwise, of materials for stockpiling in which the United States was deficient.

8. To place "counterpart funds" in a special account which could be used only for specified purposes or in accordance with agreements made with the Administrator of the United States program.

9. To publish in their countries, at least quarterly, statements of everything received under

the United States European Recovery Program.

10. To permit a United States Special Mission to operate in their countries and to have access to all information relevant to "assistance" under the act.

11. To allow United States nationals to have opportunities "equivalent to those afforded to the nationals of the country concerned," for access to natural resources in each country, needed because of deficiencies in the United States.

12. To submit to international adjudication any case espoused by the United States government involving compensation for measures affecting property rights of United States nationals.

In addition to these express conditions, it had to be understood that all purchases of certain agricultural commodities, found to be surplus in the United States, if purchased with program funds, had to be made in the United States out of surplus stocks.[28] Half of all materials procured under the program had to be shipped on United States flag vessels, subject to a very complex formula involving categories of goods and destinations designed to be sure to close all possible loopholes.[29]

A condition applicable to all forms of "aid" was embodied in entirely separate legislation concerned with East-West trade. Under the Battle Act, all forms of "aid" had to be cut off if a recipient nation sent certain kinds of goods behind the Iron Curtain.[30] The particular list of banned shipments was subject to negotiation, but naturally it always included material of direct value to the Communist war machine. One other condition that appeared for a while was the requirement that assistance be shut off for any country that was violating a treaty with the United States.[31] This was aimed at forcing France to continue special privileges for a group of Americans who had seen a pot of gold in Morocco while stationed there during the war. They convinced members of Congress that their privileges were protected by the 150-year-old treaty with the Sultan of Morocco, and that France's efforts to protect her foreign exchange rate (as required by the Economic Cooperation Agreement with the United States) violated that treaty. The controversy was not resolved until France sued the United States in the International Court of Justice to obtain a ruling on the issues.[32]

These conditions can easily be divided into two separate categories: those aimed at making sure that the program would succeed in achieving European recovery and those aimed at protecting and promoting the interests of the United States and its economy. This mixture of aims shows the confusion as to the true aims of the program. Was the United States, in providing the funds for this program, a benefactor helping other nations, or a great power helping its own interests? To those to whom such a program looked most like "foreign aid," it seemed natural to exact promises that would benefit the United States economy. To those to whom it was a measure to further the foreign policy and general welfare of the United States, only those conditions aimed at furthering the recovery of the participating countries could fairly be justified. To those who were concerned with the classical inhibitions against meddling by one nation in the internal affairs of another nation, even those latter conditions would be hard to defend. It was to them, however, that Ernest Gross addressed his remarks when he said, soon after the act had been passed, that the Economic Cooperation Agreements, containing the conditions but "freely undertaken by sovereign states," can prove to be "instruments of genuine cooperation on a scale never before attempted or . . . can bring about serious international misunderstandings and friction." [33]

In view of the extent of the conditions considered necessary and justified for the economic program, it is hardly surprising to find stringent conditions attached to the military assistance program. The most significant was the requirement of agreements designed to "assure an integrated defense of the North Atlantic Area" and "to realize unified direction and effort" with defense plans recommended by the Council and the Defense Committee of the North Atlantic Treaty Organization.[34] These conditions should have been expected; they were perfectly normal prerequisites designed to assure the success of the common defense effort. They are in interesting contrast with the provisions for military aid to China, found in the same legislation.[35] The program for China was subjected to no conditions at all, not even control over purchases, probably because the congressmen suspected that the State Department personnel who knew China best would scuttle the program. Half a billion dollars worth of supplies went to Nationalist China under this "no strings attached" policy. They remained on the mainland when the Nationalist government was removed to Formosa. Even the severest critics of the practice of imposing "conditions of aid" must be impressed with the fact that this most ineffective program of all was the least burdened with conditions, while the Marshall Plan, with its multifarious and detailed conditions, proved to be the most successful.

The question may be asked, however, whether prescribed statutory conditions are an important factor in the success of an effective program. We seldom hear that the Soviet Union has exacted explicit undertakings as conditions on which its various aid programs depend. This is partly because the U.S.S.R. has relied heavily on programs of purchasing large amounts of goods in countries where its chief aim has been "to gain a foothold in the body politic of the underdeveloped nations."[36] When the Soviet Union has begun a technical and economic assistance program, it has relied chiefly on the propaganda potential of its numerous technicians to spread the Communist word and plant the seed of revolt against Western influence. Their success has certainly been sufficiently minimal to suggest that either their ideology has too little appeal or our system of conditions is better.

In evaluating the utility of conditions in achieving the purposes of an aid program, we can, of course, disregard all those conditions not relevant to those purposes. This includes conditions aimed at benefiting the United States economy, such as the 50-50 shipping clause and the surplus agricultural commodities program. These are not really conditions imposed on the other countries, but conditions to be observed by U.S. administrators. Even if, by keeping America strong, they help to make an aid program possible, this is an incident, a by-product, rather than a primary result of the conditions. Also to be disregarded are conditions whose purpose cannot be said to further the program but which demand some performance by the other country. Examples are the Moroccan Treaty proviso and the Battle Act.

How important are conditions other than these which are not relevant to the purposes of the program? Requirements in the European Recovery Program, such as the demand that budgets be balanced, currencies strengthened, and trade barriers reduced, were all recognized by the European leaders as essentials for recovery anyway. They were always part of the OEEC program. There could never have been any possibility of our refusal of aid because of rejection of those conditions—although the European leaders often helped their own internal programs by pointing to the requirements of the Economic Cooperation Agreements as indication that American assistance would stop if parliaments or functionaries did not do their part to implement the conditions. It was only when there arose some touchy matter wholly irrelevant to economic recovery, like the traders in Morocco or commerce with Iron Curtain countries, that threats to cut off aid became serious. These were the times when our politicians had to take stock and decide whether we were furnishing the assistance essentially for our sake or for the benefit of others. The record shows how regularly the decision was in favor of continuing aid; in the midst even of a cold war, our stake is too high to let us carry out this kind of threat.

This clear conclusion may help to find the answer to the question of whether the conditions found in various aid agreements are accepted voluntarily by the recipient nations or are imposed on them through the coercion made possible by economic or military need. Like the terms to which a defeated nation submits in a peace treaty, conditions accepted under the compulsion of economic or security needs are hardly accepted "voluntarily," even though they may be considered fully binding internationally. But we have found that the conditions in aid agreements seem to have a different quality. Those that are irrelevant to the basic purpose of the program are likely to prove to be little more than window dressing, inserted to give the United States an opening to present its protests, but not really to be used as an excuse for terminating aid. Since the government officials of the recipient countries may be expected to understand this, they are not really subjecting their nations to any stringent requirements by accepting those conditions.

The conditions that are truly relevant to the purpose of the program, on the other hand, are certainly not exacted from unwilling adversaries. Except in some unusual cases, the recipients of aid have recognized the so-called conditions as proper bases for their internal policies if they are to achieve the economic or military ends mutually desired. This certainly was true in the European Recovery Program and the Mutual Defense Assistance Program implementing the North Atlantic Treaty. It seems to be so in the current Alliance for Progress, under whose charter the Latin-American countries have pledged to follow policies very similar to those found in the European Economic Cooperation Agreements. On a multilateral basis, the O.A.S. has formed a panel of experts "charged with the high responsibility of evaluating long-range development plans, reviewing the progress of those plans, and helping to obtain the financing necessary to carry them out." The individual Latin-American governments have started national development, housing, and agricultural programs.[37] These seem to be truly voluntary undertakings.

Even if the countries receiving assistance may be considered to have voluntarily accepted the conditions relevant to the program that are required by the donor government, does this mean that they also accept a full measure of supervision of the carrying out of the conditions? This kind of "donor control" comes closest to what is commonly considered "intervention."[38] Are the large aid missions, with their constant probing into the plans and policies of the beneficiaries, their publicity programs, and their outspoken criticisms, still an aspect of permissible intervention? It was interesting to hear John J. McCloy, one of the world's most experienced interveners, ask the United States Secretary of State in March, 1962, the following question:

I have a question that puzzles me, that deals with an area that I am not familiar with—very familiar with, at least—that is Latin America and this Alliance for Progress.

This juxtaposition of our aid together with land reform—how far can they fit together—what how much—how do they march together? Can we impose on a country, as a beneficiary—a potential beneficiary of our aid—a condition that they take some steps in what really affects their fundamental constitutions, their political systems? I imagine how disturbed we would be if someone was trying to press us from the outside. I just wonder if you would expand on that a little, because I have heard a good deal of comment about it.[39]

The answer to his question must lie in the same attitude that applies to all the conditions. If they are conditions that are calculated to further the common aims of a mutually agreed program, they can be looked upon as voluntarily accepted. Then the supervision and pressure that have as their purpose the achievement of those common aims are permissible forms of intervention. Conditions outside this category, however, if they are seriously enforced, stand on weaker ground. Sometimes it will be easy to distinguish between the two kinds of conditions, but in many cases the distinction will be in dispute. When this occurs, there are likely to be charges of improper interference by the donor in the other country's affairs—in other words, impermissible intervention.

Any nation prepared to furnish aid to other countries should be able to avoid such charges by channeling the aid through properly selected international organizations. While it is easy to think of economic recovery and development programs being administered by the International Bank for Reconstruction and Development, the International Finance Corporation, the O.A.S., and the like, even military aid programs will be more palatable if handled through NATO, SEATO, and especially the United Nations. In the economic field, Professors Walt W. Rostow and Max F. Millikan in their "Proposal" for economic development have described how important it is to have "a spirit of partnership . . . to avoid any suggestion of imperialist domination."[40] They conclude that "an element of international administration should enter into the proposed program."[41] In commenting on their proposal, Professor Raymond Vernon noted that they contemplate a list of conditions of a "formidable, even forbidding, nature . . . objectionable in the extreme" unless under international control and administration.[42] He also pointed out that the reactions of grantee to grantor in aid programs are not likely to be "those of gratitude or appreciation but the contrary," and an international administration can act as a buffer, protecting the principal donor, so often the United States, from "the political onus of placing pressure on aid recipients,"[43] that is, from charges of improper intervention. It would avoid what Professor Falk has called "the unreliability of a decentralized determination of when it is appropriate to intervene."[44] Those who have to deal with representatives of the other nations will find this an attractive argument, but it seldom appeals to an American congressman. As in the case of UNRRA, if there seems to be a veto or a majority vote that may defeat demands for conditions, the politicians do not like it.

And so we have the dilemma: the nation whose right hand paints itself as a generous benefactor justified in asking for certain concessions from the fortunate recipients of aid and whose left hand depicts an enlightened statesman, recognizing that a judicious sharing of his surplus assets will help to create a congenial world environment in which liberty and free institutions can flourish. It will demand the most artistic politics to enable the left hand's enlightened self-interest to keep the right hand's benefactions from causing improper intervention in the affairs of other nations.

1. *The United States and the Doctrine of Nonintervention in the Internal Affairs of Independent States,* 5 How. L.J. 163, 166 (1959).

2. McDougal & Lasswell, *The Identification and Appraisal of Diverse Systems of Public Order,* 53 AM. J. INT'L L. 1, 21 (1959).

3. Economic Cooperation Act of 1948, §115 (b), 62 Stat. 150 (1948).

4. For a description of most of them, see M. H. Cardozo, *Foreign Aid Legislation: Time for a New Look,* 38 CORNELL L.Q. 161 (1953).

5. *The European Recovery Program Agreements—A New International Era,* 19 DEP'T STATE BULL. 35-36 (1948).

6. *International Coercion and World Public Order: The General Principles of the Law of War,* 67 YALE L.J. 771, 794-96 (1958). Cf. Burke, *The Legal Regulation of Minor International Coercion: A Framework of Inquiry, infra,* pp. 87-125.

83

7. 55 Stat. 31 (1941).

8. STETTINIUS, LEND-LEASE: WEAPON FOR VICTORY (1944).

9. 62 Stat. 137 (1948).

10. See 89 CONG. REC. 8263 (1943).

11. ROSTOW & MILLIKAN, A PROPOSAL: KEY TO AN EFFECTIVE FOREIGN POLICY 132-33 (1957).

12. See WHEELER-BENNETT & LATIMER, INFORMATION ON THE REPARATION SETTLEMENT (1930).

13. See, *e. g.*, KEYNES, THE ECONOMIC CONSEQUENCES OF THE PEACE 211 (1919).

14. PRESIDENT'S FIFTEENTH REPORT TO CONGRESS ON LEND-LEASE OPERATIONS 10 (1944).

15. *Id.* at 11.

16. The text is reproduced as Appendix II of the PRESIDENT'S TWENTY-SECOND REPORT TO CONGRESS ON LEND-LEASE OPERATIONS (1946).

17. 89 CONG. REC. 8252 (1943).

18. *Ibid.*

19. PRESIDENT'S ELEVENTH REPORT TO CONGRESS ON LEND-LEASE OPERATIONS 6 (1943; earlier version, later withdrawn and amended).

20. WOODBRIDGE, UNRRA: 2 THE HISTORY OF THE UNITED NATIONS RELIEF AND REHABILITATION ADMINISTRATION, pt. 4, ch. 4 (1950).

21. 61 Stat. 125 (1947) ; 61 Stat. 934 (1947).

22. 61 Stat. 104 (1947).

23. *Ibid.*

24. 61 Stat. 103 (1947).

25. E.g., Economic Cooperation Act of 1948, §115 (b), 62 Stat. 150.

26. 19 DEP'T STATE BULL. 36.

27. Economic Cooperation Act of 1948, §115 (b), 62 Stat. 150. See Surrey, *The Economic Cooperation Act of 1948*, 36 CALIF. L. REV. 509, 517 (1949).

28. Economic Cooperation Act of 1948, §112, 62 Stat. 146.

29. Economic Cooperation Act of 1948, §111 (b)(2), 62 Stat. 143.

30. 65 Stat. 645 (1051).

31. 64 Stat. 758 (1950).

32. Case Concerning Rights of Nationals of the United States of America in Morocco (France v. United States), ICJ REPORTS (1952). See 27 DEP'T STATE BULL. 620 (1952) ; 47 AM. J. INT'L L. 1, 136 (1953).

33. Gross, *supra* note 5, at 36-37.

34. 63 Stat. 715 (1949).

35. Section 404 (b), 62 Stat. 159 (1948) ; §303, 63 Stat. 716 (1949).

36. Vernon, *Foreign Aid: "A Proposal" Reexamined,* 9 WORLD POLITICS 579, 581 (1957).

37. See *Message of the President to the Congress on the Foreign Economic and Military Assistance Program for Fiscal Year 1963,* 46 DEP'T STATE BULL. 550, 552 (1962), and *Remarks of President Kennedy to Latin America Diplomats, id.* at 540.

38. *Cf.* McDougal and Feliciano, *supra* note 6, at 794.

39. 46 DEP'T STATE BULL. 492 (1962).

40. *Op. cit. supra* note 11, at 115-116.

41. *Ibid.*

42. *Op. cit. supra* note 36, at 581. See also Falk, *supra* note 1, at 167-68.

43. *Op. cit. supra* note 36, at 584.

44. *Op. cit. supra* note 1, at 167.

The Legal Regulation of Minor International Coercion: A Framework of Inquiry[1]

William T. Burke[*]

A T A TIME when the world trembles lest an inadvertent outburst of violence by one of the nuclear powers provide the spark igniting catastrophic destruction, the problem of the deliberate use of minor coercion assumes increasing importance. The principal purpose of this brief paper is to suggest the outlines of an inquiry into the legal regulation of the less intense forms of international coercion and to raise questions concerning the community policies at stake in such regulation. The need for a framework of inquiry permitting the performance of the intellectual tasks customarily indispensable for solving legal problems is indicated by the multiple confusions that sometimes mar attempts at policy clarification by officials and scholarly observers.

Confusion stems in part from the profusion and am-

* Associate Professor of Law, Ohio State University.

biguous reference of doctrines that are offered as relevant to the problem of regulation. The main legal doctrines in customary law seem to be expressed in terms of "intervention" and "nonintervention," but there are numerous equivalents, including retorsion, reprisal, measures short of war, international tort, self-help, pacific blockade, breach of the peace, threat to the peace and so on.[2] The confusion of this prolixity of labels is of course heightened by the various shifting references ascribed to each of them.

The same observer sometimes uses a single label to designate very different phenomena, and of course an occasional similarity in labels adopted by different observers by no means implies similarity in factual or legal reference. Among the major identifiable confusions of this type are the employment of the same terms to refer to the facts of coercive conduct and to supposed legal consequences and the use of identical concepts to refer, without qualification, to both lawful and unlawful coercion. An accompanying confusion is to be seen in the common failure to attempt to distinguish between varying intensities of coercion.

The use of terminology that makes a shifting reference from facts to legal conclusions and back again is particularly evident in discussions of the key term "intervention." Observers seek factual orientation by offering definition of intervention in terms of "acts" or "behavior," but at the same time they employ the term to refer to legal conclusion. Thus the latest comprehensive study of the regulation of minor international coercion defines "intervention" as certain conduct by a state or group of states and then proceeds to refer to an alleged "right" of intervention under international law.[3] Dr. Schwarzenberger apparently envisages intervention both as conduct and as a technical legal term denoting illegality under customary international law.[4] The confusion and difficulties stemming from inquiry handicapped with such tools as these were sharply identified by Professor Grob:

> It is not too much to say that there are almost as many textbook definitions of intervention as there are of war. Almost all of these definitions, like almost all of the textbook definitions of war, are unsubstantiated. As regards the few writers who have gone to the trouble of arguing their definitions, it is easy to show that they have made one or another of the mistakes that have been made in arguing the question as to what legally constitutes war. To give an example, the fact that a certain way of conduct has been *called* intervention, no matter where and by whom, is no reason for considering it as legally constituting "intervention."[5]

Even the content of the legal conclusions supposedly connoted by such terms as "intervention" is highly uncertain. Though the latter concept is usually understood to denote unlawful conduct, that is not always the case, and the word is sometimes used by both officials and observers to signify that certain acts are permissible. On occasion the corollary term "nonintervention" is employed to define conduct as "legal," "illegal," and "extra-legal," perhaps creating some uncertainty of reference. In similar fashion some have urged that such less than precise terms of the United Nations Charter as "threat to the peace" and "breach of the peace" are useful because they allegedly carry no implications of legality or illegality.[6]

A further source of confusion in efforts at policy clarification is traceable to the failure to develop methods and indicia for distinguishing between varying intensities of coercion. None of the key concepts associated with efforts at regulation of minor coercion is in any way related to differences in the scope and comprehensiveness of coercion. Traditionally, states have sought to preserve a considerable ambiguity in the legal concepts that supposedly limit the use of international coercion, and, as a corollary, the processes of coercion to which such concepts pertain remain largely undifferentiated. Intervention, measures short of war, reprisals, blockade, and equivalent expressions have been invoked in the greatest variety of contexts, ranging from the minimum coercion in an offer of diplomatic advice to the maximum of violent military invasion and occupation. It seems doubtful, for example, whether clarification of basic community policies about regulation of coercion is assisted by employing the notion of "intervention" to refer both to a comprehensive military attack and the failure to extend diplomatic recognition.[7]

The source of much of this confusion, apart from the traditional overemphasis of lawyers upon doctrines and principles and rules divorced from the context of conditions and policies,[8] perhaps derives from the fact that, traditionally, major coercions were regarded as lawful. Prior to the conditional prohibition of major coercion established by the League of Nations Covenant, international prescriptions did not prohibit resort to war, in the sense of the most intense form of violence. There were, however, a few prescriptions that purported to govern "measures short of war," such as "reprisals," "intervention," and "pacific blockade," restricting the lawful application of minor coercion "to cases in which a prior unlawful act, or a culpable failure to perform international obligations, was attributable to the states against which coercion was applied."[9] The principal function of these prescriptions, as anomalous as they appear, presumably was to localize the use of coercion by conferring positive community approval upon a quick settlement of disputes through superior strength. The participant seeking to remedy an alleged injury could invoke such labels as "intervention" and "reprisals" as a means of signaling other participants that the object of the coercion was not to achieve a significant increment in its power position. The communication served the purpose of allaying the fears of other states and avoided the possibility of their participation in order to maintain their relative power position. The methods utilized in these "measures short of war" were frequently indistinguishable from those employed in undertakings to which the label "war" was attached.

The continued availability of these labels to justify the use of coercion became the focus of considerable attention after the promulgation of the League of Nations Covenant obliged members not to "resort to war" under certain limited conditions. The ambiguity of the term "war" seemed to place a considerable premium on the use of other terms to describe the employment of coercion. If it was only "resort to war" which the Covenant conditionally proscribed, then it might be contended, and was, that force was still permissible "if the participants used some verbal symbol other than 'war,' such as 'reprisal' or 'intervention' or other 'measure short of war,' in designating their exercises of coercion, and if they disclaimed any intention to institute a 'legal state of war.' "[10]

The Treaty for the Renunciation of War did not materially reduce the ambiguity of the Covenant in this respect, for it recorded in Article 1 the contracting parties' declaration "to condemn recourse to war for the solution of international controversies and renounce it as an instrument of national policy in their relations with one another."[11] The potential lacunae in the term "war" were, however, in the view of some commentators, remedied by the agreement expressed in Article 2 that settlement of disputes "shall never be sought except by pacific means."[12] Other observers were less confident that all measures of force were prohibited by this injunction to use "pacific means," arguing that "measures short of war" were "pacific means," even if compulsive,[13] or that force was still permissible if aimed at an objective other than settling a dispute.[14]

The United Nations Charter avoids the difficulties created by the legalistic invocation of the word "war," but the basic distinction established by the Charter between permissible and impermissible coercion has by no means quieted the controversy about the permissible employment of certain coercion. Some distinguished scholars contend that the fundamental policies projected by the Charter, the promotion of peaceful change and the prohibition of resort to coercion, require that the prohibition of coercion embrace not only the more intense forms that all admit justify the use of similar coercion in self-defense, but also the less intense coercions that might be used to remedy certain minor deprivations or violations of international law.[15] Proponents of this Charter interpretation would forbid not only the use of force which attained a certain intensity but also any other form of coercion that reached such intensity.[16] Other commentators assert that the Charter has a somewhat more restrictive compass in that it prohibits armed force of a certain intensity but does not similarly proscribe other forms of coercion having the same intensity, such as the manipulation of the economic and ideological instruments.[17]

Professor Julius Stone offers a far more limited view of the Charter prohibition of force. He appears not only to argue that lesser forms of coercion survive the Charter,[18] but that even the more intense coercion of "war" is lawful under the Charter as a response to those prior deprivations of rights enjoyed under international law that do not justify action in self-defense.[19] According to Professor Stone, for example, it continues to be lawful to employ military force for a variety of purposes other than self-defense, but especially as a means of protecting against deprivations, not necessarily amounting to coercion, that are left unsanctioned by

93

the collective community through the procedures of the United Nations. Apparently Dr. Bowett also would authorize the use of force in the event of certain lesser deprivations which he regards as threatening security, though, in contrast to Professor Stone, he justifies this by reference to self-defense.[20]

The policy justifications offered in support of these divergent positions are not dissimilar, at least in terms of long-term community objectives. Professor McDougal and Dr. Feliciano, in urging that the "prescriptions and policies embodied in the U.N. Charter forbid the unilateral use of force and violence by way of reprisal for lesser wrongs or 'tortious' conduct," contend:

> The overwhelming common interest in basic order, and the exorbitant potential costs of exercises of force by contemporary weapons, would appear to counter-balance losses states may occasionally incur from lesser wrongs left inadequately redressed because of deficiencies in available remedial procedures or the limited ability of a poorly organized community to create effective remedies for all wrongs.[21]

Professor Stone begins by assuming that the "liberty" to resort to war is still a wide one even under the United Nations Charter and urges that prohibition of resort to lesser degrees of force "may tend to drive States to seek to vindicate their claims by war, in circumstances when they might otherwise well have been content with measures less disturbing to international order."[22] The major difference between these proponents of opposing Charter interpretations may thus be seen to relate not to divergent demands about the use of major forms of coercion but to differing expectations about the consequences of resort to lesser forms of force. Nonetheless, it is obvious that the conditions under which the common interest of the community may be secured are very differently conceived. One version identifies the common interest in avoiding comprehensive violence as requiring the community to permit the use of lesser forms of coercion. In the other version this common interest is served only by prohibiting such use. If one assumes the realism of the expectations underlying one of these positions, it is obvious that a choice made according to the alternative interpretation, if made effective, could have catastrophic consequences.

Our purpose here is not to make arbitrary choice between these divergent expectations about the compatibility of lesser forms of coercion with the provisions of the Charter, but rather to suggest a framework of inquiry by which basic policies may be clarified and appropriate alternatives in community action projected for their realization. In common with other consequential problems of legal policy, it seems indispensable here to seek to illuminate the relevant process of interaction by which participants seek to coerce each other, the process of claim by which participants invoke authority for minimizing resort to coercion, and the process of decision through which authoritative decision-makers respond to the claims. Each of these distinctive processes involves certain participants, variously characterized, seeking a variety of objectives, by management of certain base values according to a great range of coercive and persuasive strategies, utilizing differing methods of interaction, claim, and decision, attaining particular outcomes and effects, and being affected by various and changing conditions. Careful orientation in these processes will permit us to distinguish facts from legal consequences and to pose issues with the sharpness of focus necessary for effective clarification of community policies.[23] After a brief survey of these processes to illustrate the kind of details that are relevant to such clarification, we shall conclude with a brief appraisal of the more fundamental community policies.

The Process of Interaction

PARTICIPANTS

All the various participants in the world social process may be seen to engage in the use of lesser coercion that has effects across state lines. The nation-state is certainly the most important actor in this process, but other territorially organized groups, such as provinces and subordinate states in federated systems and even cities, on occasion apply a significant measure of coercion. International governmental organizations, both global and regional, engage in coercive practices, more recently on an increasing scale, as illustrated by the role of the United Nations forces in the Middle East and the Congo. The transnational political party, or order, is often responsible for violent episodes that have impacts far beyond the locale of occurrence.

Private associations, especially those specialized to wealth, have been known to employ practices against each other and against other participants that impose a high degree of constraint. Even the individual human being, though of course the basic actor on behalf of every group participant, may on his own behalf control sufficient bases of power to engage in coercive strategies.

For richer indication of the type of significant detail, it is useful to survey detailed characteristics of the more important participants.

States obviously vary greatly in their total value position, especially in relative power, and it is only commonplace to note that this latter difference may alone determine the degree of coerciveness in their relationships. Variations in power position range in magnitude to such extremes that states on the lower end of the scale may command much less effective power than supposedly lesser territorially organized groups, such as cities, and less even than other types of participants, such as some private associations.

The nature of the power structure within states, particularly whether power is shared widely or concentrated in a narrowly based elite group, is sometimes regarded as an important factor affecting resort to coercive practices. Totalitarian orders, whose internal structures of authority and control exclude wide participation in the governing process, may be more likely to engage in external coercion than states whose structures permit a genuinely shared access to power. On occasion the significance of this type of internal structure has been seen in the possibility that the more

97

democratically inclined states would resort to force for humanitarian reasons.

The wealth processes within states obviously differ greatly in the degree of industrialization and in the relative importance of mineral and agricultural productivity in the gross national product. Apart from the relation of these differences to relative power positions in an aggregate sense, obviously they also bear upon the degree of coerciveness characterizing particular interactions. Though technological innovations apparently continue to outstrip scarcity of particular resources, it need not be assumed that the overwhelming balance of strength will always be with the industrialized states as it is now.

A more complete identification in this context of the characteristics of a state would also take careful note of its alliances and affiliations with other states, more particularly those alliances which associate it with competing blocs. It may be significant to take account also of the practice of rejecting certain types of alliances with other states.

By turning to other important group participants, comparable suggestions of potential details of identification could be made. It might be fruitful to consider, in the case of international governmental organizations, the regional or global character of the group, the structures of authority within the organization and its component organs, the extent to which responsibility is shared for the consequences of a group decision, and the scope of authority and control over base values made available by members.

Transnational political groups appear to merit special attention in future inquiry. Study might fruitfully take into account, in particular, the relations of authority and control between a group and a particular state, the resources available to such groups as bases of power, and the range of their operations around the globe.

OBJECTIVES

The relationship between the objectives sought by coercion and the system of public order projected by the community is most important for policy. Coercion may be exercised in support of, or in opposition to, the decisions of the organized community, and it seems indispensable to distinguish between the two very different perspectives. The common mistake of those who label collective action under the authority of an international organization as "illegal" intervention is to ignore such a distinction.

Another method of characterizing the objectives of participants which may and should be relevant to decisions about the permissibility of the coercion exercised would consider the consequentiality of the values demanded, the degree of inclusiveness or exclusiveness, and proposed extension or conservation.

The consequentiality of the objectives sought by coercion would seem especially significant for making decisions in a community that projects a system of public order based upon fundamental policies of minimizing the use of coercion and promoting peaceful change. Relevant indexes of consequentiality include the number and importance of values affected, the degree of impact upon values, and the number of participants whose values are affected in specified intensity.

The degree of inclusiveness or exclusiveness refers to the degree of participation admitted in the sharing of the values demanded. The problem is to identify the self on behalf of whom objectives are sought by coercion. The self system may extend to the whole of mankind or to a wide range of other participants or be strictly confined to the primary self consisting of a single participant.

The characteristics of conservation or extension refer to whether the participant is seeking to conserve or defend certain values or to acquire values held by others. It may be especially important to take account of community perspectives about the reasonableness of certain value positions since determining what values are regarded as "held by others" is likely to be affected by the general consensus about the reasonableness of the value position occupied.

Situations

The situations in which coercion occurs may be described by such general characteristics as the spatial position of the actors, the timing of the events in relation to other events, the institutionalization of the arenas of interaction, and the current level of crisis. The location of events may have important consequences for the possible modes of coercion available to participants including such consequences as varying calculations of effectiveness, the base values that are available for use, the objectives that the actor seeks, and the degree of importance he attaches to these goals. Timing is indicated as an important factor to call attention to the sequence of events in the total context, since the degree of coerciveness may depend not upon the alleged coercive practice itself but upon its relation to other events. The degree of institutionalization of the arena of interaction is particularly important in terms of patterns, especially whether it is organized or unorganized. It continues to be considered important whether deprivations may be prevented or redressed by reference to collective decision through established group procedures or whether the arena is so unorganized that unilateral action might appear to be the only available remedy. The prevailing crisis level perhaps bears more heavily on policy than other situational considerations. The existence of high levels of tension and insecurity obviously influences the employment of lesser forms of coercion, perhaps both to depress and to exacerbate the tendency to resort to such forms, and, as indicated previously, this factor is accorded considerable weight in contemporary policy recommendations.

BASE VALUES

People, resources, and institutions are the fundamental components of power which all participants manage in social processes. States are, of course, usually the most powerful participants in terms of control over these bases of power, but, as mentioned above, other participants may control sufficient assets to play a role equal to or greater than that of some states. Among states the differing access to base values is a fundamental condition affecting their interaction and determining the coerciveness of their relations. The unique character of a particular asset may create possibilities in coercion not open to states generally. Location on a critical strait or waterway, for example, may give a state special advantages. In such a context actions that might otherwise have slight impact could assume a highly coercive character. Other assets that have special relevance for policy include control of nuclear weapons.

STRATEGIES

The modalities of coercion, or techniques for managing base values, are commonly employed by participants in varying combination, sequence, and mutual relation to create conditions favorable to the realization of objectives. Though each of the instruments of policy —economic, diplomatic, ideological, and military—may be applied separately, the more important conception takes all into account. The principal condition sought to be created in terms of practices of coercion is, generally, the expectation of loss and the calculation that the target will be better off by conforming to the policies of the coercer.

An inquiry into the practices of lesser coercion, in

terms of the various instruments available, might reveal much of special relevance to policy. Appropriate attention would be devoted, with respect to each instrument, to participants employing it, the specific objectives sought, the targets of the coercion, the precise methods adopted, including personnel, equipment and centers and routes of operation, and the immediate outcomes and long-term effects.

Special focus on the military instrument appears justified because of its significance in the context of lesser intensities of coercion. Other instruments may of course be used to project coercion of the same degree of intensity, but the potentialities of escalation and generally increased tension seem greater in connection with active employment of military force than with other types of coercive operations.

Outcomes

The outcomes of the process of coercion refer to the varying types and degrees of intensity in coercion actually achieved. The range in intensity is obviously enormous. The availability of nuclear weapons, not to speak of bacterioligical and chemical weapons, and the development of revolutionary new guidance systems enable certain participants to approach the extreme of making the planet virtually uninhabitable or, at the least, of destroying modern civilization. Weapons of World War II vintage continue to be employed, of course, and high levels of force are still frequently attained by their use both in more episodic situations

103

and in those of considerable duration. At the same time increasingly refined techniques of infiltration and subversion, sophisticated measures for manipulating the flow of goods and services, and improved methods in symbol dissemination and communication permit increasingly fine, but highly effective, gradations in the application of coercion. And accompanying all these forms are the innumerable types of pressure and constraint that are an inevitable feature of a world arena whose major participants are highly unequal in both aggregate and particular value positions.

The relevance of all these varying intensities of coercion to the appraisal of the lawfulness of minor coercions is obvious. Authoritative community policies and prescriptions already provide standards for identifying major coercion, general criteria for determining the permissibility of such coercion, and procedures for coping with impermissible resort to force. But the position of minor coercions is not so clear. It is questioned, in the first place, whether such coercions ought to be considered impermissible at all. If so, it is uncertain whether contemporary policies and prescriptions provide adequate criteria for distinguishing minor coercion from the ordinary coercion associated with normal interstate behavior or establish with sufficient explicitness a satisfactory range of remedial procedures.

EFFECTS

The critical nature of the long-term consequences of resort to coercion consists, beyond the destructiveness of the particular instance, in the possibility that even the exercise of a lesser form of coercion may trigger catastrophic violence. The bases for this view lie, no doubt, in the apprehension that nuclear weapons technology will soon be within the reach of a considerable number of states, in the likelihood that more advanced delivery systems will increasingly become available beyond the small circle of states now possessing them, and in the general instability characterizing a system built upon such complex and rapidly changing technology. In light of these expectations, it is thought by some that states have much less to lose from enduring those deprivations to their interests that do not threaten important bases of power than from respond-to these lesser deprivations with minor, but perhaps forceful, coercion.

A completely different set of expectations is entertained by those who contend that in the long run suppression of resort to minor coercion would tend to make comprehensive force more likely. In this view the current state of affairs is characterized by a collective security system that is not effective nor likely to be so, by a preference for peaceful change which unfortunately is not translated into techniques by which such change may be achieved, and by a set of economic and social conditions that lead to constant change and friction inflicting more or less serious deprivations, though less than the use of force, upon state interests. As a result of these factors, it is suggested, a state may suffer considerable injury that the existing system remains completely unable to remedy through collective procedures. If the individual state is also forbidden to resort to minor coercion in self-help, the accumulation of irritations and pressures may create conditions favorable to the employment of very intense forms of coercion.

Conditions

Though the context in which coercion occurs obviously does not remain static, and features relevant to one instance of coercion may have no relevance with respect to another, certain conditions may be emphasized as especially important. These include the rate of population increase in certain areas, the increasing interdependence of peoples around the globe, the tendency toward a multipolar arena, and the emerging crystallization of identifications among some elites with regard to symbols of past domination. A fuller treatment would indicate the detailed relevance of these trends for expectations of coercion, but even brief consideration suggests the possibilities. The continued and growing disparity between the size of the population and productive potential in certain states creates extremely favorable conditions for resort to coercion. Increasing interdependence does not necessarily entail co-operation for securing values, since recognition of the same condition may also facilitate the imposition of deprivations. The recent deceleration of the tendency toward bipolarity and the emergence of a multipolar arena, in which several states possess the capacity to employ devastating force, may create moderating tendencies as recognition increases of the gravity of even limited coercion in such an explosive context. On the other hand, an apparent identification system incorporating newly independent states, but formed around the wholly negative rejection of historical forms of domination, may create occasions in which major powers are tempted to interfere. For example, the recently proclaimed approval by some states of the use of force to eject a "colonial" regime may have very unfortunate consequences.

The Process of Claim

Our major concern here is to achieve a categorization of probable claims and counterclaims which will help us to clarify goals, describe and project trends, identify conditions, and recommend alternative policies.

States are the major claimants invoking community authority, but other participants very frequently have resort to processes of authority to remedy the effects of alleged unlawful resort to coercion. The objective of claimants is, of course, to secure the prescription and application of authority for restraining and coping with the harm caused by the coercive practices.

Types of Claims

The initiation of coercion occasions two very different types of claims relating to major and minor coercion. The former, more important claim, with which we are not here concerned, is that the coercion employed reaches such an intensity that it threatens important bases of power of a state and both permits the use of substantial responding coercion in self-defense and authorizes the organized community to activate the processes of collective security. The counterclaim usually alleges that the coercion employed was itself in the exercise of self-defense. These claims about major coercion are usually considered in terms of "aggression" and "self-defense" and are associated with a whole cluster of derivative claims to which the law of war is a response.

The other category of claims embraces those relating to the maintenance of minimum order when minor coercion is employed. The more important claims here are (I) the claims relating to the permissibility of minor coercion and (II) the claims relating to particular sanctioning goals.

I. The claims relating to the permissibility of minor coercion

The principal claim is that certain coercion has been or is being employed which does not reach such intensity as to constitute major coercion but which is still unlawful and gives rise to certain sanctions. The complementary claim, asserted in opposition, maintains either that the coercion is not impermissible under international law and does not give rise to sanctions, or that, though otherwise impermissible, it is itself a lawful sanction in response to a prior unlawful deprivation.

The assertion that a particular minor coercion is

impermissible invokes prescriptions embodied in customary international law and in the United Nations Charter. The Charter provisions relied upon include the negative prohibition in Article 2(4) obliging members to refrain from the use of force and the positive injunction in Article 2(3) to settle disputes by peaceful means. In customary law the familiar prescriptions, as dark in reference as they may be, are those pertaining to intervention, nonintervention, and international torts or delinquencies, including treaty violations, property deprivations, and other lesser coercive acts.

The complementary claim that resort to minor coercion is permissible may of course be that the activities in which the state engages are inevitable in the day-to-day interactions of states and do not amount in scope and intensity to prohibited coercion. Other probable claims are that the instances of permissible use of minor coercion recognized in international law before the U.N. Charter continue to be lawful and, in particular, that Articles 2(3) and 2(4) do not extend to complete prohibition of all forms of coercion other than that employed in individual or collective self-defense. The state is entitled, it is accordingly urged, to rely upon prescriptions of customary international law such as permissible reprisals and permissible intervention. This argument may be supplemented by the allegation that the exercise of forceful measures of self-help is fully within the community's expectations about the sanctions permissible under contemporary international law and that the United Nations Charter may be interpreted appropriately to reflect these expectations.

It seems obvious that an appropriate inquiry into these conflicting claims about permissibility cannot be organized in terms of the legal labels invoked in justification. An outline of claims that possibly would escape this ambiguity and permit performance of the necessary tasks might be of the character set forth below. The object of the outline is to permit inquiry into both the subjectivities of actors and their operations (coercive acts). A principal subjectivity is that the actor employs coercion deliberately for achieving an objective. This (hopefully) excludes inquiry into events involving unintentional deprivations, such as accidents and other unforeseeable contingencies.

A. The claims that minor coercion is impermissible

    1. Minor coercion unaccompanied by allegation of prior coercion
    The inquiry would consider the relevance of certain factors for past decisions in terms of phases of the process of interaction.

    2. Minor coercion employed in response to prior unlawful conduct

B. The claim that minor coercion is permissible (Same subheadings as in previous claim.)

All the factors in the process of interaction outlined above are of course relevant in the clarification of community policy unique to each type of claim as well as in surveying previous decisions and examining the factors that have affected them.

II. Claims relating to particular sanctioning goals

The significance of the claims relating to the five sanctioning goals listed below is to facilitate the survey and assessment of the many different sanctioning practices and techniques invoked with regard to the varying intensities of coercion in different contexts. It will be observed that each of the sanctioning goals is related to a different sequence in the process of international coercion.

A. The goal of prevention

Claims about prevention concern measures to be taken in advance of any particular instance of coercion and involve practices designed to create conditions favorable to persuasive strategies.

B. The goal of deterrence

Claims about deterrence are those to invoke collective and other procedures of settlement as a method of deterring imminent use of minor coercion. The focus would be on demands for resort to international organizations, courts, and arbitral tribunals to forestall less persuasive means of settling disputes.

C. The goal of restoration

Claims to restore public order are those made

to secure community intervention, or to act unilaterally, in order to repress the employment of coercion.

D. The goal of rehabilitation

After coercion is terminated, claims center upon the measures available for reparation of the values damaged or destroyed.

E. The goal of reconstruction

Claims are also directed at the longer-term objectives of modifying structures of authority in both internal and external arenas. The object is to provide arrangements for creating perspectives that facilitate the use of persuasion in seeking value changes.

The Process of Decision

DECISION-MAKERS

The officials established by the constitutive process of decision to resolve conflicting claims about the use of minor coercion are the same as for other types of claims. They include international governmental organizations, the judges of international courts and tribunals, and the officials of nation-states. The latter are, because of the nature of the arena, still the most active and important decision-makers. It perhaps bears emphasis that state officials participate in decisions irrespective of their participation or non-participation in the coercion process.

OBJECTIVES

The overriding goal for which international decision-makers are established is that of minimizing resort to coercion. The various subsidiary goals through which this major goal is sought include prevention, deterrence, restoration, rehabilitation, and reconstruction.

ARENAS

Claimants seek to invoke community authority processes in a variety of arenas, including those that are internal and external in relation to particular states, those maintained for exercising authority functions on a continuing basis and those established for dealing with specific instances of coercion, and, finally, those arenas that exhibit organized and unorganized patterns of authority. The arenas within a state are of unusual significance with respect to minor coercion since provision of opportunity for access to internal decision processes may have considerable effect upon resort to coercion in response to alleged lesser deprivations. Arenas which are both organized and in continuous operation are similarly important for the possibility they afford of resort to collective decision as a means of redress. Traditionally the international community has lacked a significant degree of organization, and this has had great impact on decisions about the permissibility of resort to minor coercion. Although the functions of authoritative decision in the world community have in the past decades become more institutionalized, there continues to be considerable decentralization in the decisions about the use of coercion. As will be seen, this lack of effective procedures for collective decision-making still bears importantly on policy.

Base Values

Decision-makers differ greatly in the values at their disposal for supporting the performance of authority functions. International governmental organizations, though accorded the not inconsiderable basis of power implicit in the grant of authority from states, still depend chiefly upon the support of member states for control over consequential assets. And when all authority functions are considered, as indicated in the outline of outcomes below, the international organization wields greater aggregate bases of power than might otherwise appear to be the case. Such organizations have at their disposal, more or less unfettered, useful military forces, a great range of skills, the active loyalties of their agents, a considerable capacity for gathering intelligence, and a surprising array of channels of enlightenment.

The officials of nation-states usually, however, control base values of far greater magnitude than other decision-makers and obviously can employ them in support of unilateral, and in rejection of collective, decision. Even this preponderance of power may serve public order, of course, when these bases of power are used to sanction choices guided by criteria of common interest. Calculations about the willingness of other

114

states to employ their assets to support community decisions about the use of minor coercion have great impact upon the willingness of one state to commit support to collective decision, and such willingness, accordingly, has significance for policy.

STRATEGIES

The methods available for managing base values in support of a decision about the use of minor coercion include all the instruments of policy—diplomatic, economic, military, and ideological. The traditional emphasis has been upon diplomatic strategies, as suggested by the reliance, unsuccessful for the most part, upon such methods of peaceful change as negotiation, conciliation, mediation, and arbitration. One of the fundamental weaknesses of the decision process is, of course, that military strategies are not frequently available to support collective decisions.

OUTCOMES

The decisions made by officials about the permissibility of minor coercion include all the policy functions, but the more visible, critical phases of the decision process are the prescription of policy, *i.e.*, the projection of general regulations, and its application, *i.e.*, the characterization of particular conduct in terms of conformity or noncomformity with a regulation.

The prescription of policies about minor coercion evolves through both the customary shaping and development of a general consensus in the community and the procedure of explicit agreement. Custom is responsible for most of the doctrines about minor coercion, though more recently, of course, community prescriptions are to be found in comprehensive agreements such as the Covenant, the Pact of Paris, and the Charter.

The application of policy, especially the employment of minor coercion as a sanction, is also associated historically with unilateral action by individual states. The fact that very recently states have sought to institutionalize the use of coercion as a sanction has, of course, created doubts about the permissibility of employing such coercion as a mode of self-help.

Though the sanctioning efforts of the United Nations have not been a spectacular success in terms of repressing violence already initiated, the organization's efforts at prevention and deterrence represent substantial, if insufficient, progress. Such progress may be measured particularly in the many international programs directed at alleviating conditions conducive to resort to coercion. States acting independently of the group are also contributing substantially to this effort, though the motivation is perhaps related more to political advantage than to sanctioning goals.

EFFECTS

The longer term consequences of the flow of decisions about minor coercion embrace not only the distribution of particular values, and not only the kind of compre-

hensive public order the community establishes—
whether compatible with human dignity or not—but
even whether any human community is permitted to
survive in recognizable form. The increasing delicacy
of the balance of terror by which a precarious "peace"
is maintained perhaps is too fragile even to endure the
multiple shocks of resort to minor coercion. There are,
thus far, few signs of willingness among the officials of
major states to make explicit arrangements that will
strengthen the procedures for isolating and confining
these episodic resorts to lesser coercion.

CONDITIONS

Among the factors not already mentioned, those that
have, or may have, an important impact on decisions
about permissible minor coercion, are changes in the
relative strength of the various contending world public
orders, the emergence of new systems of public order,
changes in interdependences and in their recognition,
changes in the techniques of major and minor coercions,
the expectations of particular decision-makers about
the probable effectiveness of their choices, and estima-
tion of costs involved in making and enforcing a choice.

Clarification of Policy

Clarification of the community policy he recommends
is the first essential step of the scholar concerned for
promoting effective community action in control of

coercion, just as it is indispensable for making decisions in an arena which projects the goal of maintaining a minimum public order. If minimum order is to be secured, or meaningful steps taken to this end, it is necessary to appraise particular exercises of coercion in terms of their conformity to the goals of public order and, where the coercion does not conform to such goals, to initiate sanctioning measures appropriately designed to cope with the situation. The object of the present brief statement is obviously not to achieve this clarification in detail but rather to suggest basic, overriding goals and to indicate questions which might lead to a more meaningful detailed clarification.

The basic complementary policies at stake in the regulation of minor international coercion derive from the United Nations Charter and from the unavoidable exigencies of a world community still largely without effective organization for the collective enforcement of important international policies. On the one hand the goal is to achieve effective implementation of basic Charter objectives: the promotion of change by peaceful procedures and the prohibition of resort to coercion except in self-defense. On the other hand, in an arena that is effectively decentralized in making decisions about redress of wrongful conduct whose effects do not warrant the exercise of force in self-defense, it may be necessary to regard as authorized some resort to coercion as a sanctioning measure designed to protect against harmful, if lesser, deprivations. The goals as thus conceived appear to call for prohibition of coercion, whether or not responsive to prior illegal conduct, which seems from the perspective of the disinterested observer to have a serious potential of expanding to a high intensity, as measured by the number of participants, the scale of coercion, its duration, and other factors. Impermissibility would, in short, embrace coercion of an intensity less than justifying the use of force in self-defense, *i.e.*, coercion that does not directly threaten important base values, when in the context it appears probable that more important bases of power may become targets. Minor coercion would otherwise continue to be permissible, in response to prior illegal conduct inflicting serious harm, insofar as it is reasonably necessary to secure redress and not disproportionate to the injury received. Obviously the prior illegal conduct might itself be an impermissible use of minor coercion.

The more detailed problems for policy are, initially, to consider the factors that decision-makers should take into account in appraising particular coercion in terms of these goals and, then, to consider factors relevant to the choice of remedial, sanctioning measures to be directed at nonconforming coercion.

The first of these tasks calls both for distinguishing minor coercion from major and ordinary coercion and for considering factors relevant to distinguishing between permissible and impermissible minor coercion.

The significant distinctions between minor coercion and major or ordinary coercion are identifiable in terms of certain characteristic subjectivities and operations. Major coercion, identifiable as the intent to use intense coercion to attack important bases of power (subjectivities) and the actual attack or threat of attack upon such bases (operations), is of course prohibited by the United Nations Charter, except for self-defense. Ordinary coercion is seen in the pursuit of lawful objectives (subjectivities) by means of acts which have but slight coercive impact (operations). The particular subjectivities of minor coercion may be considered to include the deliberate use of coercion against components of a target's value position other than its important bases of power, and the operations consist of acts of considerable but not high intensity of coercion.

The key variables to be taken into account in distinguishing between degrees of coercion in terms of subjectivities and operations include all phases of the process of coercion. In seeking to survey the total context of coercion, one might, for example, consider the weight to be attached to such factors as the detailed identification of participants, particularly their relative size and strength, whether the goals sought are highly valued and whether the object is to conserve or acquire new values, the characteristics of the situation in terms of location and time relation to other events, the specific base values controlled by participants, the significance of the combination of coercive instruments employed, especially the military, the specific coercive impact of the acts involved, and the long-term effects on community values.

The determination of the impermissibility of a particular minor coercion calls for assessment of the same key variables from the perspective of determining both the probable immediate and longer-term consequences of the resort to coercion and the relation of the responding coercion to the prior unlawful act. Such a survey would entail consideration of all phases of the coercive process to determine first whether attacks on important bases of power might reasonably be expected as a consequence of the initial resort to coercion. Perhaps the factor of distinctive importance here is the modality of the coercion, especially whether military force is applied in any significant measure. The grave probability of comprehensive destruction already appears too high to permit states to have recourse to substantial military violence as a means of redressing deprivations for which the community does not provide an effective remedy. Special weight might also be attached in this determination to the alliance or bloc with which a participant identifies and the public order systems brought into conflict. Clearly the nature of the objective is a critical consideration since, for example, any use of coercion for acquiring values might be considered impermissible. Whether the purpose is to use coercion to oppose or support community policies and decisions is obviously also a basic factor. Among situational factors, the location of participants, in relation to major power centers for example, may strongly affect possibilities of expanding the scope of coercion. The importance of time may be seen in the duration of the coercion or in whether the coercive acts stem from a long-term exclusive policy or represent an immediate response to events. A discrepancy in particular base values may provide a clue to the subjectivities of the actors, as in the inferences about the consequentiality of objectives that may be drawn from failure to rely upon especially potent bases of power. The outcomes of the coercive acts in terms of the kind and degree of destruction of values actually achieved may be an essential consideration in projecting consequences.

The final task in the appraisal of permissibility in resort to minor coercion would be the consideration of the coercion as a response to the prior unlawful act. Again reference could be made to all phases of the process of coercion to determine, by reference to the total context, whether the original harm inflicted serious or inconsequential harm, whether the response was or was not proportionate, and whether alternative remedies were fully explored.

The most difficult policy problem, not treated here, is that of assessing the factors relevant to the choice of sanctioning measures in response to non-conforming coercion. All phases of the process of authoritative decision would be considered in detail in a rational choice of sanctions. The specific problem, however, is to consider and assess the detailed practices that can be employed or that may be devised for preventing outbreaks of minor coercion, for deterring imminent use of coercion, for restoring order after coercion has occurred, for rehabilitating value patterns disrupted by coercive practices, and for reconstructing the system of order in ways designed to avoid future coercion.

1. I wish to acknowledge a substantial debt to Professor Myres S. McDougal of the Yale Law School, for his assistance on this specific problem. It is apparent, in addition, that

I have drawn heavily from the general intellectual orientation and framework of inquiry elaborated by Professor McDougal and Dr. Florentino P. Feliciano in their study of major coercion. See McDougal & Feliciano, Law and Minimum World Public Order (1961). See also Lasswell and Kaplan, Power and Society (1950).

2. See generally Grob, The Relativity of War and Peace, ch. 2 (1949) ; Briggs, The Law of Nations 958-60 (2d ed. 1952) ; 2 Hyde, International Law 1654-78 (2d ed. 1945).

3. Thomas & Thomas, Non-Intervention 71, 74-78 (1956).

4. I Schwarzenberger, A Manual of International Law 272 (4th ed. 1960).

5. Grob, op. cit. supra note 2, at 227.

6. E.g., Stone, Aggression and World Public Order 21-26 (1958).

7. Virtually all of the foregoing confusions are illustrated nicely by Professor Fisher's paper *Intervention: Three Problems of Policy and Law, supra* pp. 3-30. In classic demonstration he uses the term "intervention" to refer without discrimination to both major and minor coercions, as if no differences in law or policy, to use his distinction, turn on varying intensities in the actual exercise of coercion. On other occasions the term is apparently intended to express legal conclusion, principally to imply illegal action (pp. 8-9), though legality is not necessarily excluded by referring to a situation as "intervention" (pp. 19-20). One confusion mentioned in the text above that Professor Fisher tries especially, but unsuccessfully, to avoid is that concerning the legal "rules" relating to the use of force. Though he thinks that "there is much room for discussion," he finds that "the basic rules of international law are reasonably clear" (p. 7). Unfortunately, this supposed clarity of legal rule fails to survive even his own analysis for he subsequently announces that "we shall have to clarify the rules beyond the basic propositions stated above" (p. 14) as well as "develop criteria for distinguishing" internal revolution from external interference (p. 14), and, finally, he submits, "we should not forget . . . the lack of any standards for defining intervention . . . ." (p. 15).

123

8. Professor Fisher again provides convenient and wholly adequate illustration of these tendencies. He cautions us not to identify law with policy in this context and urges us especially not to equate lawfulness with reasonableness (*id.* at 3-4). Perhaps I might caution against the uncritical acceptance of such views by indicating some of the misconceptions that underlie them. Chief among them are the suggestion that a policy-oriented approach to jurisprudence precludes any useful resort to legal rules; the notion that law consists solely of a body of "rules" and that the lawyer's task is merely to discover the "rule" and lay it before the decision-maker; the belief that inherited rules provide always but one answer to a controversy, removing any necessity for choice between competing principles, policies, and sets of values; the question-begging assumptions about the inclination of courts to apply the "law as it is", accompanied by simplistic statements purporting to describe how decision-makers behave; the contention that it would "produce disorder" if international decision-makers were to apply a standard of reasonableness by measuring the permissibility of their conduct in terms of criteria established in accord with the common interests of states; and, finally, the intellectually sterile suggestion that it is important to distinguish the systems of the "domestic scene" from the "international arena" because in the former "we have a government of laws and not of men."

[The editor has kindly shown me the two new footnotes above and allowed me a brief note in response. There seems little reason to explain the quotations taken out of context from which Mr. Burke constructs a straw man—a nineteenth-century straw man at that.

Professor McDougal has properly been concerned with questions of process, and with the role to be played in that process by objective norms. As I see it, the task of the present papers is to seek useful ways of thinking about the problems involved when one country takes action which another may regard as "intervention." I find it more useful to try to suggest a few new general criteria for decision than it is to inventory and catalogue some of the almost limitless factual variables to which McDougal has previously called attention.—*Roger Fisher*]

9. McDougal & Feliciano, *op. cit. supra* note 1, at 137.

10. *Id.* at 140.

11. 4 HUDSON, INTERNATIONAL LEGISLATION 2524-25 (1932).

12. 2 OPPENHEIM, INTERNATIONAL LAW 184 (7th ed. Lauterpacht 1948).

13. *Id.* at 184.

14. STONE, LEGAL CONTROLS OF INTERNATIONAL CONFLICT 286 (2d rev. ed. 1959).

15. McDOUGAL & FELICIANO, *op. cit. supra* note 1, at 207 n. 193.

16. *Id.* at 142-43.

17. See, *e.g.,* GOODRICH & HAMBRO, CHARTER OF THE UNITED NATIONS 104 (2d ed. 1949).

18. STONE, *op. cit. supra* note 14, at 288.

19. STONE, *op. cit. supra* note 6, at 92-103.

20. BOWETT, SELF-DEFENSE IN INTERNATIONAL LAW 23-25 (1958).

21. McDOUGAL & FELICIANO, *op. cit. supra* note 1, at 207-8 n. 193.

22. STONE, *op. cit. supra* note 14, at 288.

23. The contexual orientation offered here is adapted from that employed for analysis of policy problems arising from the exercise of major coercions in McDOUGAL & FELICIANO, *op. cit. supra* note 1, *passim.*